I'LL

TAKE

MANHATTAN

THE SQUATTERS' PROJECT

MAXIMIZED SPACE

Two plays by Carole Di Tosti

OTHER WORKS BY CAROLE DI TOSTI

NOVEL
Peregrine: The Ceremony of Powers

POETRY BOOK
Light Shifts

PLAYS
The Berglarian
The Sicilian Lighthouse

THEATER AND FILM REVIEWS
(On the following sites)
Sandi Durell's Theater Pizzazz.com
Blogcritics.org
Carole Di Tosti's NYC Skyline

ESSAYS/OPINION PIECES
The Fat and the Skinny on Wellness.com

WEBSITE
www.caroleditostibooks.com

I'LL TAKE MANHATTAN

THE
SQUATTERS' PROJECT

MAXIMIZED SPACE

CAROLE DI TOSTI

I'll Take Manhattan
Published: December 2024
Printed in the United States of America
ISBN: WILL ADD

For my New York City Friends

(who helped me get through COVID-19)

CONTENTS

THE SQUATTERS' PROJECT

1

MAXIMIZED SPACE

77

ACKNOWLEDGEMENTS

The Squatters' Project and *Maximized Space* have never been produced. *The Squatters' Project* was conceived in Eduardo Machodo's playwrighting class with revisions under his guidance. Eduardo Machado is a globally renown playwright, who has written over 60 plays, TV and film scripts, as well as a food memoir with Michael Domitrovich. He is a director, actor and professor (Columbia University, NYU, Sarah Lawrence College, etc.). Check out his biography on https://en.wikipedia.org/wiki/Eduardo.

The Squatters' Project received a reading under the guidance and assistance of Eduardo Machado at Theatre for the New City (Crystal Field, Artistic Director) with the participation of the following actors: Kennath Raboy, Heather Velazquez, Amelia Gwaltney, Stefan Diethelm, Drew Valins, Michaela Lind and Hugo Fernando Aleman.

Maximized Space was conceived in playwrighting teacher Julie McKee's class at HB Studios. When COVID-19 interrupted live classes, we reverted to Zoom. I completed Act I. However, I became redirected, overwhelmed by the first pandemic in the history of my generation. I left off writing *Maximized Space*, and to negotiate my rage at how COVID-19 was being "managed" and botched by 45, I wrote two other plays about the pandemic, *Pandemics* and *Nosferatu of the Pandemics*.

Pandemics received two readings in workshops at HB Studios and ESPA (Einhorn School of Performing Arts). It also received a reading on Zoom with actors from Westchester

Collaborative Theatre. *Pandemics* is an examination in real time of New York City during COVID-19, up until the election. *Nosferatu of the Pandemic* was successfully workshopped in Julie McKee's playwrighting class at HB Studios. The satire is a farce about vampire bats that contract an equivalent of COVID-19, which threatens to exterminate their species.
Writing *Pandemics* and *Nosferatu of the Pandemic* helped me overcome the stress and fear of the pandemic. Also, it prepared me for Eduardo Machado's playwrighting class where I was able to write *The Squatters' Project* and extensively revise and update *Maximized Space,* which takes place in New York City in February-March of 2020.

Like *The Squatters' Project, Maximized Spece* received a reading under the guidance and assistance of Eduardo Machado at Theatre for the New City. The following actors participated: Stefan Diethelm, Amelia Gwaltney, Kiara Luna, Charles Manning, Jody Moore and Emmett O'Connell.

I also would like to acknowledge the Tyrone Guthrie Centre at Annaghmakerrig, in Ireland for their support of my writing in their returning residency program. Because of the inspiration and encouragement that I've received from fellow residents encompassing all arts areas, I've been able to evolve in my writing and publication. I am forever grateful for the staff at the Tyrone Guthrie Centre Annaghmakerrig House, who help to provide a place where creativity flourishes, and for the nation of Ireland, whose unflagging support of the arts continues to inspire me.

THE

SQUATTERS'

PROJECT

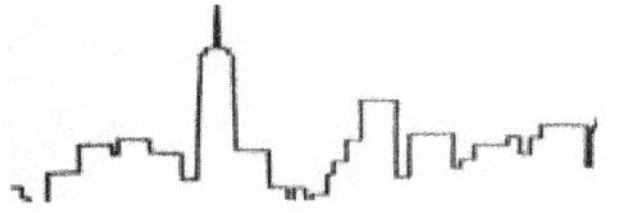

CHARACTERS

THE PRINCIPALS

The four principals are all New Yorkers from the boroughs or LI. They are middle class who have been "radicalized" in various colleges in one way or another. They were into drugs and free love, then had to support themselves.

MARJORIE, legal secretary, 1970s activist, college radical, Rally's BFF (20s)

RALLY, insurance broker, 1970s activist, college radical, Marjorie's BFF (20s)

MICHAEL, NYC sanitation worker, met Peter through family ties (28)

PETER, freelances construction in the family business, mentored by a family lawyer (26)

THE SQUATTERS' PROJECT

The Squatters' Project are members who helped originate the squatting community.

SAM, a founding member whose receives guidance from the Beach Channel Squatters (30s)

HEDDY, a founding member and sentinel of the community squats (30s).

THE ANTOGANISTS AND THEIR CREW

The two antagonists live in New York City and have ties to organized crime.

RYDER DANIELS, hired agent provocateur for the 5 families, no college (20s)

LOLITA, Ryder's partner, secretary and confidante, some college, named herself (25).

Two slackers Ryder recruits with pot to help him and Lolita.

FRANK, a druggie who roams the area and is always ready to smoke pot. (23)

JUAN, Franks' friend who is clueless about the squatting community's mission (20)

SETTING

TIME: Fall 1975

PLACE: Lower East Side, Manhattan, New York

ACT ONE

Scene 1

1970s Lower East Side hole-in-the-wall coffee joint

MARJORIE Why do you always need to be in love with someone?

RALLY I need sex.

MARJORIE Intimacy. You crave intimacy

RALLY Yes, intimacy…and sex.

Michael enters.

RALLY Hi, Michael. (*She hesitates.*) I asked Michael to join us. We need to discuss something. I think you'll be pleased.

MICHAEL You'll be pleased, Marjorie.

MARJORIE Now, everyone's thinking for me. Do I have a choice?

MICHAEL We have a proposition for you.

MARJORIE I know where this is going.

RALLY No, you don't.

MARJORIE You tried this on me once before.

MICHAEL That wasn't a sure thing.

RALLY This is solid.

MARJORIE If it involves an investment, it's no.

RALLY More important than an investment. But it will bring a sizable profit.

MARJORIE Is it that building that's a wreck? Not interested.

RALLY Not to buy it.

MICHAEL Not yet.

MARJORIE The place is dangerous, falling down.

RALLY It's perfect for squatters. Nobody wants it.

MARJORIE Janice, who's in the movement, told me folks squatted for a day. Terrible stench of death, so bad they left.

MICHAEL I've checked city law, squatters' rights. You can take hold of property very easily.

MARJORIE With no electricity? No functioning toilets?

RALLY For toilets? Go to a café or public bathroom.

MICHAEL We have a lawyer who is working with us.

RALLY You have to be homeless and establish the place as your residence, then occupy it, until it is!

MARJORIE Who owns the building?

RALLY Whoever. He owes the city and the state back taxes and fines. Friends told us the city put it up for auction.

MARJORIE Do I know these friends?

MICHAEL The ones I'm talking about are hardline advocates. They're taking a stand against homelessness and landlords who treat renters like scum. We've joined them. Taking on the banks and the city. Establishing a squatters' community. There'll be an elder and artists' center, housing, all D.I.Y. Exciting, right?

RALLY If we succeed, we'll move to other bombed-out sections of the city. Show how it's done. Super Squatters who hold landlords accountable.

MICHAEL Slumlords make millions exploiting the poor and chiseling the city out of tax dollars. They don't fix heating or plumbing. If the city goes after them, they abandon their buildings and burn them. They've stoked the city's crime wave. We say, "Not on our watch!"

MARJORIE What does your lawyer say?

RALLY Two words. (*pause*) Adverse Possession.

MICHAEL Enough to send chills up the spines of Scumlords. Speaking of lawyers, we want to keep ours on retainer.

MARJORIE (*pause*) Will those hardliners accept you?

MICHAEL Think so. Too late. I just gave up my rental.

MARJORIE Crime, gangs, white flight, no city resources—

MICHAEL (*interrupts*) The activists will accept us if there's co-squatting. We have to join now, 'cause there's others looking. We can't let them occupy before us.

MARJORIE How are you going to live with no indoor plumbing?

MICHAEL I work sanitation. I'll clean up at home base. Any unwashed stench will blend right in. Ha, ha, ha.

RALLY It's a noble cause. We're pioneers. Decades from now, New York won't be just a shit hole that went bankrupt thanks to that bastard, "Drop Dead Ford!" He did us a favor. Our community model can be set up in run-down areas here, there, everywhere.

MARJORIE When you said stuff to me a month ago, I wasn't interested because I'd have to leave my apartment—

MICHAEL (*interrupts*) No. You're the stable one. It's Rally and me who are the ones who will take possession.

RALLY We camp out, sleeping bags, lanterns. Cook with a coal stove. Bottled water. Someone has to be there day and night. It's harder when they send surveillance teams. You can't leave. So, we're getting married.

MARJORIE Ah, ha. Now I get the sex and intimacy thing.

MICHAEL What?

RALLY Nothing. So, I'll stay and write about the movement—

MICHAEL And I'll work and join her evenings.

RALLY There must be a book deal somewhere in it for me.

MARJORIE New York winters? You'll freeze, get pneumonia, die—

MICHAEL Why are you so negative? We need your support. You've been close to Rally your whole life. Trust her.

RALLY Remember, "Up the People?" Remember, "Our rights, whatdaya say? Corporations have to pay!"

MARJORIE You're flying without instruments in a whirlwind, the pilot's unconscious and everyone's screaming "LAND THE PLANE." Anything can happen. People kill people for land and property.

RALLY We are putting our lives on the line. But it's for the social good. Home ownership is a slow war against the middle class. The upkeep of the money pit. Mortgage stress. The pressures give ya chronic illnesses you die of. With squatting you live on the edge. And build something meaningful with friends, become a community.

MICHAEL (*pause*) The lawyer will write up the contract to credit your sweat equity. Every hour, every dime you spend holding the building for the community counts.

MARJORIE What this blows up? Where's my sweat equity then. If lose the building, I have nothing.

RALLY There are squatters out in Beach Channel, waterfront property. Ya know, those old summer bungalows that were abandoned cause no one wanted to pay the taxes. The community got together and are toughing it out. No toilets or central heating or electricity. They stopped the city declaring eminent domain. Stopped developers. Stopped the bulldozers leveling the sheds. They stopped the rich bringing in their friends and throwing out the middle class. They claimed it as theirs. They pushed the city to an agreement. The deal to give it to them is finalized. The process works.

MICHAEL If!! If you work the process. They played roulette and they won.

MARJORIE You're caught up in your own euphoria. I'm a realist. I have to see it before I'm playing Russian roulette.

RALLY Time and again, the city used eminent domain to move out the little people. They put them in projects and justified their racism. They pointed the finger and said, "Get a job." In Harlem, the Bronx. Lincoln Center. The Rockaways. Developers want tenement buildings razzed, so they can buy the dirt and raise up rich peoples' condos. Not so fast. The squatters are here. We're protesting for families. Black, Hispanic, everyone whose been closed out of housing.

MICHAEL If you squat the buildings, that's 80% of it. Brick by brick we create housing with dignity and respect. It's a return to communities with neighbors sharing our most fundamental needs. How we live. How we connect. How we help each other. When they see we're like the Beach Channel squatters, there'll be resistance. We're confronting homelessness, and discrimination. We're destroying someone's profits for affordable housing.

MARJORIE Housing IS everything. No home, you don't exist.

MICHAEL Housing isn't the only thing that's everything. Money answers all things. We need your financial support to live there and renovate. This isn't a haphazard act. We have to establish a legal foundation, so the city can't demolish it and give it to the banks.

MARJORIE This lawyer. you trust him?

RALLY We got his name from the Beach Channel squatters.

MARJORIE It's easier "sitting on the dock of the bay, watching the tide roll away" instead of waking up in the dark with rats gnawing your face.

RALLY They can't condemn a building if someone's claimed adverse possession. Please come to the lawyer with us.

MARJORIE Is there three-way ownership?

RALLY We put in the physical work. You put in money for lawyers' fees, court filings, whatever. Michael's salary will help. You're the sweat equity.

MARJORIE I don't know.

RALLY We've been friends forever. I never steer you wrong.

MARJORIE You'll be married. I'm an intruder.

RALLY Not if we each take a third of the property.

MICHAEL We do the rats, the cold, no plumbing, and the danger. You do the easy part. We'll need a gun for protection.

MARJORIE What about saving money, getting a loan and buying?

MICHAEL Who can afford the interest payments? We'd be living hand to mouth, while banks get fat off our interest dollars. They'll own our souls, like the company store in a West Virginia mining town.

RALLY Squatting is the people's right in an unaffordable market.

MARJORIE And what do they say about fighting city hall?

RALLY Where's your idealism? You were the Queen of Protests.

MICHAEL Let's see the building, then go to the lawyer.

Peter enters

PETER (*excited*) Hey, guys. We're beginning this evening.

MICHAEL Peter. You're here, now? But we're not ready.

MARJORIE I have to run.

MICHAEL Peter, this is Marjorie. She's interested.

MARJORIE Don't put words in my mouth.

RALLY We're going to the building, then Siegelman.

PETER I have the ground rules from Siegelman. You don't need to see him. And I heard disturbing news.

RALLY What?

PETER Another group is moving in today or tomorrow. We have to claim our living space now.

MARJORIE This is where I get off.

RALLY Don't leave, Marjorie. We'll go there now.

PETER I'm the point person on this. Who are you, exactly?

MARJORIE Nobody that matters.

PETER You friends of these two?

MARJORIE Rally. We go back a long way.

PETER Rally's a rebel, not your white, middle-class chick. Feminist marches, the Viet Nam War marches, Kent State, Orange Sunshine, hash, mushrooms, free love.

MARJORIE Ha, ha, ha. Guilty.

PETER Ha, ha, ha. You're not a fan of unaffordable housing that's causing poverty and homelessness and crime. The middle class deserted our city of dreams. But we still dream. This is a great opportunity. We're taking ownership of their derelictions. We're occupiers—

RALLY (*interrupts*) We just told her the razzle dazzle.

MARJORIE An idea whose time has come. But I'm not an activist.

MICHAEL Everyone's an activist. Just because you have a steady job doesn't mean you're not. The protest went underground. You're an iconoclast like the rest of us.

PETER All types make up our community. But you've got to have a building first. Let's get ours. I have padlocks and I dropped off a load of materials for repairs.

MARJORIE I thought you said that it was just the three of us.

RALLY I thought so too. Hey, Michael?

PETER Michael and I have been doing the legwork for months.

RALLY You're a lawyer?

PETER I'm great at interpreting legalese. On the way I'll tell you the city, state and federal laws that help.

MARJORIE So now there's four of us? That means we each have one-quarter share of the building. We need a contract.

MICHAEL We do the hump work. You provide sweat equity dollars.

PETER Hump is my name. I know carpentry, dry wall, plumbing, electric, heating. I'm street smart and legal smart.

MICHAEL Glad we ran into Peter. Saved me telling you.

RALLY What the hell, Michael? Keeping secrets is shitty.

PETER I'm saving your asses.

MICHAEL Peter's great. You've heard me talk about him.

RALLY No.

MICHAEL The other day. I said there's this guy who'll update us on the problems we'll face. Didn't say his name.

RALLY Is this the troublemaker that they were talking about?

PETER I'm him. That group is political. Dirt for brains.

RALLY Are you gonna be a problem with them?

MICHAEL Not if you don't make it one.

MARJORIE I'm heading out.

RALLY Please, don't. I need you to pair off with.

MARJORIE (*interrupts*) You're already a pair.

RALLY That's just, that's, I mean I need a friend, a female friend in this with me. I can't trust anyone else.

MICHAEL What are you saying? You can't trust me?

RALLY Not if you tell lies of omission.

MARJORIE This is getting too complicated.

MICHAEL Peter is the rock. He'll be there when the going gets rough, the back up on the back up.

MARJORIE We need a contract with conditions and escape clauses. That way someone breaks it, we hold them accountable.

PETER Of course, mademoiselle. You can back me up with legal matters. You sound like you have a head for it.

MARJORIE I know.a few things. Doing pre-law.

PETER We'll partner up. Shake on it? Take my hand.

MARJORIE That will leave you with only one.

RALLY Ha, ha, ha, Psych.

MICHAEL Come with us to see the lawyer tomorrow. We'll set up the contract. You're our second point person.

RALLY You owe me Michael. Don't pull any more surprises on me or I may be the one to walk.

MICHAEL A divorce before we're married?

RALLY (*deadpan*). Ha, ha.

PETER We'd like the pleasure of your company in our glorious adventure. We're going to steal back what the Sheriff of Nottingham has taken from us peasants these past decades. We must brook him no quarter. May we count on your brilliant presence to accompany us to the castle?

MARJORIE Ha, ha, ha.

RALLY I can't believe you want to begin now. It's afternoon.

MICHAEL Not a moment to lose, if we have to get more stuff.

PETER Let's go. I don't want anyone to take my toolbox.

RALLY But I was gonna make a list.

MICHAEL Make a mental list. Well, Marjorie?

MARJORIE I guess I have to see this castle.

PETER It's a fortress against corruption. Today we're superheroes working the dream, shaping reality.

Lights dim as the play continues into the next scene.

Scene 2

The stage is in darkness, except for Rally and Marjorie's flashlights. The third floor is a mess with old boards, bricks, garbage, debris, stripped walls. The wrecked floors and sets should be stylistically suggested. There is the sound of hammering and voices offstage.

MARJORIE Who would want to compete with us for this disgusting hell hole dump? Uhhh. What is that smell?

RALLY We could never do this without the guys. Never.

MARJORIE The first floor is a mess. Second floor is gone. This is the best floor of the three and it's a disaster. The building should be torn down. We're idiots to try.

RALLY We have to take it over today. The Beame administration is too flooded with complaints and humiliated by the federal government to do anything to stop us.

MARJORIE I don't see anyone else in the area or on the street.

RALLY Michael says others have staked out their claims on streets less run down. This place is the worst.

MARJORIE You should have started a month ago when we spoke.

RALLY We didn't know enough.

MARJORIE YOU didn't know enough. Peter and Michael knew a lot.

RALLY I don't know what I don't know. He didn't tell me.

MARJORIE Usually, you share something that important with me.

RALLY Not always.

MARJORIE If you hadn't been so secretive about Michael, I might have been persuaded. We'd have a better building.

RALLY Now you say that? You weren't interested.

MARJORIE You were holding something back. Your relationship with Michael was tied up with the building.

RALLY He didn't want me to say anything because he was checking things out.

MARJORIE The bold grab their luck. He was weak. Dragged his feet. You lost valuable time. Got the shittiest one.

RALLY Michael said nothing. I'm fucked up about it.

MARJORIE That should be a warning. What else is he not saying?

RALLY It's why I want you in on this. A warning sign is going off in my head. I need alone time to talk to Michael.

MARJORIE I don't think you'll get all of the truth from him.

RALLY That's a lousy thing to say.

MARJORIE I'm honest. I'm not afraid to tell you to go fuck yourself. If I've been afraid in a relationship, I messed up because I couldn't take the truth. Then it came and bit me in the ass. Bam!

RALLY I don't know if I can be honest with a guy.

MARJORIE That's fear talking. You have to confront Michael's secrecy or get bitten in the ass.

RALLY Now's not the time.

MARJORIE Why not? Do you really love him?

RALLY I'm going with him into this building thing, aren't I?

MARJORIE The building is a separate issue. Don't let him put the two things together. That's confusing.

RALLY If you love someone, you work things out. right?

Sounds of steps on the stairs. Peter and Michael enter.

PETER Don't go on the second floor. You'll fall to the first. The supporting beams are sagging. Stick to the edges. Load bearing walls are weak. Place needs an overhaul.

MICHAEL We put new boards on the stairs of the ones that gave way. The stairs are strong. Forget the second floor.

MARJORIE Do you know what you're doing?

PETER I've been reading a bunch of books on construction. Summers I work with my uncle in his business.

RALLY What kind of construction. Houses? This is a city dwelling. Totally different.

MICHAEL The principles are the same.

PETER The point is for now, don't go on the second floor unless you want to break a leg or get a concussion or put your eye out. There are exposed nails where folks tore out floorboards to set a fire. Don't ever walk bare foot. And wear shit kickers. The place is booby-trapped with nails, dead mice, bugs, filth, lead paint, who knows what else. Get a tetanus shot. I did.

RALLY Jesus Christ.

MARJORIE I'm not coming here alone. I'll end up killing myself.

MICHAEL You won't kill yourself if you do what we say.

RALLY Squatter neighbors are blocks over. We'll go to them.

MARJORIE Not if they're our enemies. They could just let us bleed to death if we fall through the second floor…

PETER I told you not to go on the second floor.

RALLY You and I will come here together, and we'll make sure the guys are here. Peter will be here all the time. We have to get him everything he needs since he's doing the scut work and Michael's helping.

MARJORIE You know I haven't agreed to anything. And after finding out the horrors of this dumpster pit, I'm probably going to back out.

MICHAEL We've plotted the safe and unsafe areas. Second floor off limits. Third floor, better. But you have to feel your way around to see if the boards are solid. Be ready for anything. Ha, ha.

MARJORIE How can you laugh? Our lives are over, if we fall to our deaths. And, and, what about the roof crashing down on our heads! This isn't going to work for me.

PETER The roof is leaking, but it's the one thing the previous owner seemed to take care of. The tarring is about ten years old. So, the city must have been on top of him for that. Then things got out of hand.

MICHAEL The lawyer is looking into what was repaired until the former owner walked away. Right, Peter?

MARJORIE   It's a crime no renters brought the bastard up on charges. Or maybe they sued, and he stiffed them. Everyone walked away. Even the city. What a tragedy. It was a cool building once. Meanwhile, there are people who have been evicted from their apartments and need places to live. And they're on the streets.

PETER   The reason why the second floor is so bad is cause that's where the owner set the fire. But those old beams were oak or maybe treated with something, so they never really caught. They don't make 'em like they used to. The fire department was on it. But there's enough damage to make the center weak.

MARJORIE   You know I'm not staying here. (*pause*) Don't look at me like that.

PETER   No, no. I get it.

RALLY   Neither am I.

PETER   The fragile damsels. ha, ha, ha, ha.

MICHAEL   Peter stays for the first few months, makes it safer.

PETER   My first priority is the second floor.

MARJORIE   I'll stay when you get the heating systems working.

PETER	**MICHAEL**
Ha, ha, ha	Ha, ha, right away.

MARJORIE   What? You're acting like heat isn't coming for years.

PETER   It isn't. That's one of the last systems to go in.

MARJORIE   I can't do this. This isn't a fortress. It's your pipe dream. It's easier to get a loan and buy a house.

RALLY You won't be buying a house in Manhattan.

PETER A loan? You're paying eight times what a property is worth when you're done. Banks are criminals. They don't care if you can't make the payments. They'll wreck your credit and take all your equity. You have city and state property taxes. And if you can't pay, they'll take the house and put it up for auction to get the back taxes. You have to come up with a hefty down payment to buy and if you don't have credit, ladies, and you probably don't, you're fucked. Daddy has to co-sign. You default? He's screwed.

MICHAEL With the taxes and city services going up and inflation? Every day you fear default. No way to live.

RALLY None of us can afford a three story, even here.

MICHAEL Squatting is the way. So you deal with physical hardship for four years. The movement helps you. What you've built has more value than a material structure. Lifelong friendships, lifelong family, community.

MARJORIE I can't be here at night. If I decide to go in, I'll help when I can, but I'm not sleeping with rats and bugs and cold. And where do I pee if I have to get up in the middle of the night? No plumbing, toilets.

PETER You pee in a bucket you empty out back in the morning.

MARJORIE Like Solzhenitsyn's poop bucket in his book, *Gulag Archipelago*? Jesus! This is the 1970s, not the 1930s.

RALLY At least we won't get shot to death by Soviet prison guards. Ah, ha, ha. You guys are lucky, whip it out, pee in a bucket or in the yard. We can't hold it, or we get infections. I'm not squatting over a bucket—

MARJORIE Now I know where they came up with the name "squatters." Ha, ha, ha. You squat to pee, then trip over the bucket and spill it in the night. Ah, ha, ha

Others laugh.

MARJORIE (*interrupts*) Oh, wow! Spilling pee. That could be a good thing. If wolves don't like human pee, maybe rats won't either, and they'll stay away.

MICHAEL We don't expect you to sleep here overnight! At first.

PETER Let's talk security. I reinforced the front door with heavy duty padlocks. They'll have to find another squat to break into. I've got a rifle. I put my stuff in the back first-floor apartment. Back door's secure.

MICHAEL Tomorrow, after we see the lawyer, I'll stay with ya. Are you ladies thinking lists?

RALLY	**MARJORIE**
Yes.	No. I'm feeling sick.

RALLY I have some water left.

MARJORIE No water. I need sunlight. Air. This is a dungeon. (*breathes heavily*) I have to get out. I have to—

MICHAEL (*interrupts*) Watch out. Be careful. Let me help you.

MARJORIE I want to be outside. Have to get out. OUT! OUTTTT!

RALLY She's having a panic attack. Just sit down and get your breath. Then go with Michael.

MARJORIE Now, now! I feel faint. Faint! EWW I SMELL RAT PEE.

MICHAEL Be careful. Stop swaying. I got you. We'll go. Slowly, move toward the wall. Hold onto the wall. Calm, slow…

MARJORIE Uh oh. The room is spinning. Uh. Uh ewwwwww. Bluckkk

MICHAEL Don't puke. Don't puke. Hold it. Not on me. STOP!

MARJORIE (*shaking, vomits*) There's a rat over there. Aich!! I can't hold it! Yak, Yak Yak, BLUCKKKK!!

RALLY There's no rats. It's your imagination. Just breathe.

MARJORIE There it is. I see it… ARGH! Yak Yak, Uhhhh

PETER I'm shining a light on the stairs. Hold onto Michael.

RALLY Breathe through your nostrils. Watch out! She'll fall through to the first floor. WATCH!

MICHAEL SHUT UP! I got her. She won't fall.

MARJORIE Let me stand here and breathe.

There is loud continuous banging on the front door.

MARJORIE WHAT??? Ahhhhhh! No, no, no.

MICHAEL Wait. let go, let. me, I'm falling.

Michael and Marjorie fall overhanging the stairs.

MARJORIE Fuck, fuck. OWWWW. *OWWW OWWWWW*

MICHAEL I said watch out. What. Christ. FUCK!

MARJORIE You made me fall. ARGGHHH!! Get off. OFF!! OWWW!

MICHAEL Owwww. Owwww. Stop kneeing my balls. Owww. Owww. Careful. Don't push me down the stairs.

MARJORIE OWWWWW MY BUTT. Go. Go. Off. OFF

The banging gets louder.

PETER What the hell?

MARJORIE ARGH.My ass bone.MY ASS BONE.AGGGG

MICHAEL Shit, Bastard. Sorry! Sorry!

RALLY It's the police. Too bad the windows are boarded up. We could see if there's a squad car.

MARJORIE My ass bone. AGGHH. splintered. ARGH!!

PETER SHUT UP. Don't SCREAM. They'll hear. Muzzle her.

RALLY Come on, Marjorie. Shut it.

MARJORIE (*high pitched whine*) MMMMMMmmm

MICHAEL I'll help you up. (*pause*) They know we're here—

MARJORIE Let me get up on my own. I'll shut up. If you jerk me around, you'll make me scream again.

VOICE OVER (RYDER) Open up! We know you're in there!

PETER Shhhhhhiiittttt.

RALLY We have to see who's at the door.

MICHAEL (*whispers*) Can't do that now. We wait until they get tired and go away.

PETER (*whispers*) I hope they don't go around back. The doors aren't secured. I was gonna put some locks and boards after you left. FUCKALL. FUCK! FUCK! FUCK!

RALLY They're ripping the boards on the front door!

VOICE OVER (RYDER) Open up it's the police. OPEN UP. We're breaking in.

MICHAEL (*loud whisper*) We're sitting ducks. They're going to smash the padlocks.

MARJORIE Ahhhh! ARGh! I broke my tailbone. Fuck me. It' knives in my ass if I try to get up.

PETER. SHHHH. At least you're not dizzy and puking.

RALLY (*regular voice*) One of you has to go down.

VOICE OVER (RYDER) You can't trick us. You left the car on the side street. OPEN UP before we wreck your locks.

PETER Me or you, pal?

PETER	**MICHAEL**
You	You

RALLY I'll go down. I'm the female. I'll play coy.

VOICE OVER (RYDER) You're in violation. It's an abandoned building.

MICHAEL I'll come with you.

PETER Me too.

MARJORIE Someone has to stay with me. I can't move. You have to scare away the rats. They're gonna bite me.

PETER Rally, you stay.

RALLY My plan will work. I know how to flirt with cops.

MICHAEL Peter, don't let them know you're here. Rally will take care of the cops. I'll be next to the door.

PETER	**MARJORIE**
All right.	Smart thinking.

Rally and Michael go downstairs.

RYDER Open the door! Open it! OPEN! IT!

RALLY (*opens door slightly*) Where are the cops?

RYDER I represent The Lower Eastside Vigilantes. You're in violation. You have to let me in. I'm an inspector.

RALLY Where are the other vigilantes?

RYDER Come outside on the stoop. You can see them down the street. Down there. (*points*) See?

RALLY You're a SCAMMER. You're trying to get over. Get the fuck out of here. You're not the police.

RYDER Why are you so nasty? How many of you are there?

RALLY None of your business.

RYDER We need to know, cause you don't belong here.

RALLY I'm homeless. I belong. I have nowhere else to go.

RYDER Why here? There are a ton of other places in the city.

RALLY It's empty. I'm homeless. It's a good fit.

RYDER It's occupied. You have to leave.

RALLY If you're a vigilante, where's your red cape and hat.

RYDER I said L.E.S. Vigilantes. Not Guardian Angels. I'm monitoring things so the building isn't taken over by outsiders who break city laws.

RALLY Who're the others? I want to meet them.

RYDER They're checking other houses.

RALLY Bring them now, or I'll think you're here to attack me.

Michael pushes the door wider and stands next to Rally.

MICHAEL And that would be really stupid, cause by the looks of you, runt, I'll beat your ass. Either get the fuck out or get your posse.

RYDER I'll compromise. Just a few questions. You make any changes? You're homeless? When are you leaving?

MICHAEL No compromise. No answers. Who the fuck are you?

RYDER Ryder Daniels. You just got here and you're bossing me around? Don't push this into a standoff or you're out. You're trespassing. And when the others come, you tell us what we want to know, or we evict you.

RALLY Ryder Daniels, we're not the enemy. Banks are the enemy. They want the property for nothing, so they turn it around for a cool million. You're vigilantes? It's perfect. We're squatters. Protect us.

RYDER I am.

MICHAEL Busting up the boards on the front door? Threatening us with eviction? Great protection.

RYDER I have the right to tell you what's what. You have no rights on this land.

RALLY You're just like the banks. Fucking hypocrite. We have the right of possession of an abandoned building.

RYDER It's occupied.

MICHAEL By us. No one else is here. You're too late.

RYDER You didn't occupy it.

RALLY You don't know what we did.

RYDER I know because you got here today. And our spies said you parked the car on the other street.

RALLY Wheee. You got spies.

RYDER You're leaving at dusk 'cause you aren't equipped to stay overnight. You leave your car on the streets? It'll be stripped. Ha, ha, ha, ha.

MICHAEL You don't know shit.

RYDER That's why I'm here. I want to know shit. Who are you? Who's with you?

RALLY None of your business, and none of your business.

RYDER We're the local law enforcers. If you're with the movement, you have to let me in. If you stonewall me, it's a mistake you don't wanna make.

RALLY No one owns this property. We're here now. You start violence, we get the cops.

RYDER The cops don't come to these streets. They're afraid.

MICHAEL Are you trying to say we should be afraid?

RYDER Cops don't come down here. It's dangerous. The lights have been shot out. The city left us in darkness. This is the forbidden zone. The city's in trouble. They're worried about where the money for paychecks is coming from. Until Ford bails out New York, no cops, no construction, no street sweeping, no garbage pickup—

MICHAEL (*interrupts*) These streets look kept up.

RYDER So, where do you stand?

MICHAEL Right here.

RALLY Same as before.

RYDER You can't stay, unless you show me what you've done. Did you make any changes? They need to be recorded.

MICHAEL Why?

RYDER If somebody dies because of shit getting out of hand, it could jeopardize the whole movement. If squatter deaths make *The Daly News* headlines? It'll start a bureaucratic horror show. We'll all be evicted.

RALLY That's the first thing you've said that makes sense.

RYDER This building is scheduled for someone else.

MICHAEL Who?

RYDER Not you.

MICHAEL Where are they? We've asked you to bring the other vigilantes and you're still here arguing?

RALLY Bring them and we'll talk. Otherwise, goodbye.

RYDER Don't! Shut! The door! I have to look around.

MICHAEL You're trespassing. It's ours and no one says it's not. Sorry, in someone's imagination it was theirs. But the reality is, we occupy it.

RYDER I came in peace. I warned you.

RALLY I don't call your attitude peace.

MICHAEL If you came in peace, why didn't you bake a cake or bring bagels and coffee to show your good will.

RALLY Bring the bagels tomorrow and bring enough for a celebration. Then we'll talk.

RYDER You have enough flashlight batteries for tonight? You have other boards? I just wrecked this one. My posse's comin' we'll rip 'em up and throw you out—

MICHAEL *(interrupts)* How do you know I don't have a shotgun laying up somewhere inside? You destroy the door, you're breaking and entering. You threaten my girl, I protect her. Flesh wounds aren't guaranteed. I hit an artery; you bleed to death.

RALLY He's not a violent man, but I can't be responsible for what he does if I'm in danger. You're not bullying and threatening me in the daytime, the nighttime, anytime.

RYDER I'm not bullying you. I'm telling you facts.

MICHAEL You can't lawfully act like you own the streets. You're not a cop. This isn't the wild west, and no one made you sheriff. The building is public property, gone off the tax rolls. No one wants it except for a group on the fringes of society. This is our property in a community like no other. You wanna discuss it, come back tomorrow, bring good faith or don't show your face around here again.

RALLY Easy Ryder, ah, ha ha, ha. Be Easy. You catch more flies with sugar than vinegar. And sometimes you need flies, you know? Sometimes flies are great for getting rid of rotting flesh. The maggots eat the rot—

RYDER What are you on drugs? I'll be back.

Ryder leaves. Michael shuts the door.

RALLY Shit. Let me secure the padlocks—

MICHAEL (*interrupts*) We've got to repair his damage. Go Upstairs. Tell Marjorie and Peter.

The scene continues upstairs.

PETER Not sure about the doctor.

MARJORIE I have radiating pains down my leg when I move off my ass. I know I broke something. I need a doctor.

PETER Wait and see.

MARJORIE Fuck you—

PETER Go to the ER.

MARJORIE Then I'll need an ambulance, E.M.T.

PETER They're not coming down here. You're on your own. You know that list you're supposed to make? Add first aid kits, a medic bag, fire extinguishers.

Rally enters.

RALLY We have to make some decisions fast.

PETER She's going to the ER

MARJORIE   I need X-rays. I broke my assbone. I can't get up.

RALLY   Same thing happened to my little cousin. Slipped on her butt in a pool. X-rays, no X-rays, it has to mend on its own. You don't need a doctor or ER.

MARJORIE   I have to see a doctor to set the bone with pins—

RALLY   You can't put pins in a tailbone. It's like a rib. It's probably a small fracture. They hurt the worst.

Michael enters.

MARJORIE   How do you know? That was your little cousin. I'm an adult with an adult assbone. My bones are bigger. X-Rays will tell what's going on.

MICHAEL   No X-rays. If we leave, we lose the building.

PETER   What? How?

RALLY   Neighborhood squatters are going to grab this place out from under us. We can't leave. They think it's just me and Michael. He told them he has a gun.

PETER   Told who?

MICHAEL   This Ryder guy.

MARJORIE   You have to carry me downstairs. I can't walk. I'm in a lot of pain. I have to go to the ER.

RALLY   We're being watched. We leave, they'll break all the boards on the front door, bust the padlocks, change them and take over our squat. Just take an aspirin.

MARJORIE   Aspirin? Are you crazy? I'm going to the ER. Bring the car around and you guys carry me downstairs. I'm not staying a minute longer in this horrible dungeon.

RALLY Pipe down. Let me think of a plan.

PETER I don't get it. What did the guy say to you?

MICHAEL They'll take the house out from under us. The boards have to be repaired where he busted them. And we need more padlocks.

RALLY I have an idea. Let's bluff them. Let's make them think we left. But first we fix up the door. Then—

MARJORIE (*interrupts*) What about me? I need to go to the ER.

MICHAEL Shushhhh. Rally, finish what you were saying.

RALLY You, me and Michael drive to the ER, after we fix the doors. Peter stays out of sight, just like he was going to later this evening to protect the place.

PETER Yeah, but I don't have all the stuff I need.

MARJORIE Who's talking about lists now? You said you had it.

PETER Not all of it. I could use some chains, and ah, other stuff. I got the boards. They're on the first floor.

MARJORIE You come off sounding like the expert, so prepared. What other stuff? Huh?

MICHAEL No time to deal with your bitchiness. This Ryder character is going to bring his gang. He threatened to come later. Maybe he's fronting. (*pause*) Maybe not.

RALLY I never thought I'd say this, but you may have to use that gun to protect this squat against them. What is it Peter, a rifle?

PETER A hunting rifle somebody gave me. And I don't fucking know how to use it.

MICHAEL   All you do is just squeeze and a round goes off. What's so fucking hard?

PETER   I don't have any ammunition.

MARJORIE   GREAT! Gee, let me put that on the list—

RALLY (*interrupts*)   Oh, Mr. Big Man. (*mimics*) I have a rifle.

PETER   I didn't think the first night we're here I have to use it. Remember, we heard they would be coming for this building tomorrow.

MARJORIE   Let's go! It's crashing symbols up my ass! Come on!

RALLY   How can you be such a klutz? You play tennis, swim. Take the aspirin. If I find them (*searches bag*).

MARJORIE   It was an accident, his fault. I got tangled up and I fell the wrong way 'cause of his BIG, HUGE LEG—

MICHAEL (*interrupts*)   This is going nowhere. How much do we want this house? What are we willing to do to keep it?

PETER   You know the answer. But we need an emergency plan. Or it's gonna slip through our fingers. You were supposed to stay with me, Michael. I don't want to be here alone at night without ammunition.

RALLY (*holds out her hand*)   Take these. Four of them.

MARJORIE   I don't have water. You have water? I'll choke. EWWW.

RALLY   I finished the water. Do it! The guys will repair the boards on the front door. I'll bring the car around. Chew and swallow, NOW! Less pain going downstairs.

MICHAEL   We leave, they'll know that Marjorie is with us. And we're couples, a dead giveaway. They'll assume there must be another guy hiding inside.

RALLY   You don't know. Maybe they'll think we've left if we bring out somebody injured. Maybe they'll assume we're not coming back and we've given up.

MICHAEL   I think Ryder is scamming us, but I want to think that. You want to think they'll assume we've given up and wait until tomorrow. What if they come tonight?

MARJORIE (*choking*)   Disgusting. Torture. I can't swallow them.

PETER   I'm not gonna be here alone, tonight, to face off a gang without a weapon.

RALLY   Don't be a baby. Then, spit it out and take the pain.

MICHAEL   You'll be OK, Peter if this Ryder guy is bluffing.

PETER   If he isn't?

MARJORIE   We're just going around in circles. I chewed the aspirin. Go get the car, Rally.

RALLY   You chewed all of them?

PETER   What if they show up before you get back?

MICHAEL   Ha! Do like they did in the Wild West. Hold 'em off.

PETER   You did boxing. You should be here not me.

MICHAEL   Stay in the back of the house. Don't answer. They go away and come back tomorrow. Then they face all of us.

MARJORIE I'm not staying.

RALLY We'll come back after we pick up stuff. We'll stay.

MICHAEL We can't stay the night with the car on the street. Ryder said they'd strip it. What do we do?

PETER Marjorie, swallow them. You're holding us up.

MARJORIE I took two. I can't get these others down.

RALLY I'm getting the car. Hope they didn't mess with it.

MICHAEL Didn't think of that. My mind is frazzed. Careful on the second floor. Go down the way you came up. We need more flashlight batteries. We'll be in darkness.

RALLY I'm rethinking things. Don't count on me. Marjorie probably can't drive to drop us off. I'm going to have to go back to the apartment, Michael.

MICHAEL Then, hurry up.

MARJORIE Aren't you guys going to help me down the stairs?

PETER I've got to repair the front door. Michael help her.

MARJORIE But I'll need both of you. I'm in a lot of pain.

MICHAEL I'm helping Peter with the doors. The aspirin will kick in. You'll be able to go it alone.

PETER Take the aspirin, Marjorie, for Christ's sake.

MARJORIE Fuck you. (*She takes a pill.*) I have no saliva left. The other pills ate it up.

MICHAEL I'm boarding up the back door. No padlocks.

PETER Too dangerous. That leaves only one way out. If there's a fire, we're fucked. We need chains and—

MICHAEL (*interrupts*) Just for tonight, Peter, in case we can't get the chains later. (*over his shoulder*) You'll be OK, Marjorie. Stay put. We'll be on the first floor.

Peter, Michael and Rally go downstairs.

MARJORIE (*yells*) Very funny. Where the hell am I going? (*long pause*) Ohhhh! (*pause*) What's that? What? Where is that coming from? (*panicking*) No, no no. Ahhhhh! You MOTHER FUCKER. I SEE YOU. ARGHH! Get the hell out of here. Get! This is MY TERRITORY. OUT! OUT! What can I throw at you? What do I have? Here, you bastard! Here. You're nothing but loose change anyway. Ha! Ha! Pennies. How's that? Ha! And quarters. Here's another. And Another! AH, HA, HA How does that feel? Stings, right? Ah, ha, ha. Oh. Jesus Christ. Fuck. This fucking flashlight. The batteries? Oh, come on. Not NOW! Don't. It's coming on. Whew (*pause*) Oh, Fuck no. Fuck No! Fuck me. Fuck me (*screams*) ARGHHH! I WILL NOT BE LEFT IN THE DARK WITH RATS. No! No. No. No. Take your fuck out of here! Two of you? GET THE FUCK AWAY. ARGH! Gotta leave. LEAVE. GOTTA GET OUT. ON YOUR ASS MARJORIE. On your ass. MOVE. DOWN THE STAIRS. Go, go, go, go. Go. Go, go… oh. Fuck me. Fuck me. Did you bite me you MOTHERFUCKER? NO! NO! (*yells*) PETER! MICHAEL! HELP! PETER! MICHAEL! PETER!!! MICHAEL!!!

MICHAEL (*far away, from first floor*) What?

PETER (*from first floor, yells*) Shut up. The whole neighborhood can hear you screaming your piss out.

MICHAEL Come with me Peter.

We hear Michael on the stairs.

MARJORIE   GET UP HERE! RATS. Rats! A fucking herd of rats. HELP!

MICHAEL   Need your flashlight on the second floor. Peter!

MARJORIE   Rats. Swarming. They're biting. Hurry. HURRY.

MICHAEL   On the second. Coming. Peter get up here. COME ON!

PETER   One fucking thing after another. I gotta finish the fucking door. I have to stay here tonight. You do it.

MARJORIE   They're on me! The CLAWS. HELP!! MICHAEL! HELP!

PETER (*yells up*)   You're wasting time. She's OK.

MARJORIE   The rats! Rats! CLAWS. THEY'RE SCRATCHING! BITING.

MICHAEL   Coming to the third. Where are you?

Michael arrives with the flashlight.

MARJORIE   Oh. Light. I never thought I'd LOVE LIGHT!

MICHAEL   You OK?

MARJORIE   NOOO! There's more than one. I threw coins and, the batteries died and, I got bit. And I PEED myself

MICHAEL   I don't see rats.

MARJORIE   Behind me, to the left. All over.

MICHAEL   I'll BRING THEM OUT.

MARJORIE   NO! LET THEM STAY. They'll SWARM AGAIN.

MICHAEL Peter! Come up here. We've only got the one flashlight.

MARJORIE Peter! If you don't come up here, I'm gonna scream bloody hell and bring all the squatters.

PETER (*angry*) She's a mess. Crazy! Shut the fuck up.

MICHAEL Careful. We don't want more injuries.

Peter enters.

PETER Here's light. Whew. Out of breath.

MICHAEL If there's a rat problem, you need to know.

MARJORIE There's more than one rat. There's a fucking colony. And I'm not going to be their food. If you're staying, tonight, you'll be dinner. Ha, ha, ha, ha

MICHAEL Shine your light back there, where I've got mine.

PETER Nothing there. Nothing! Don't tell me you brought me up here for the drama. We don't need your DRAMA! Shit!!

MICHAEL I don't see anything. Nothing's there. Let's go.

MARJORIE Of course, there isn't with you stomping up the stairs and flashing the lights. They went into their holes. They're in the building. Must be 50 or sixty of them.

MICHAEL Hmm. Only way to really tell is look for the droppings.

PETER And big, rat droppings. Not mouse turds.

MARJORIE I've never been so scared in all my life.

PETER It's just a fucking rat.

MICHAEL Peter. Bring the light over here. Look. There's a pile of rat shit. It's their toilet.

PETER Oh God. Yeah. That's more than one rat. That's.

MARJORIE You thought I was hallucinating. Oh. the hysterical female.

MICHAEL Well, they're not stupid. They're on the third floor where it's safer. Not the second where they could fall through and break their necks.

PETER Rats don't have necks.

MICHAEL Necks, no necks, it's bad. A shit pile's here, too.

MARJORIE You have any extra batteries?

MICHAEL Peter? Any extras?

PETER You were gonna get them, if you ever fucking leave.

MARJORIE Well, if you're staying overnight, flashlights aren't enough to scare them. You missed the rat turds in the kitchen, I bet. Sure you wanna sleep there? Ah, ha, ha.

MICHAEL We didn't even finish working on the doors. Rally's going to be here soon.

PETER Let's go downstairs.

MICHAEL Do you still have pain?

MARJORIE Ha, ha, ha. The rats scared me painless. I can go down on my butt. But second floor landing's full of holes.

MICHAEL We need both flashlights. We'll go before you. Come down on your ass. slowly.

MARJORIE Maybe I can stand.

PETER No standing. No standing. Just sit your way down.

MICHAEL Let's go. Slowly, slowly.

PETER (*interrupts*) Oh, man. The rats are watching. I see their beady eyes. A ton of them.

MARJORIE You're scaring me. I panic, I fall. Shut up.

PETER Yesh… there's more than two of them. In a pack they're dangerous. Hurry, hurry, they're gonna rush us.

MICHAEL Pick up the pace. Pick up the pace. Pick it up—

MARJORIE Asshole. I'm not a wussy female. I know the rustling of rat claws on wood. Slower. Don't get ahead of me.

PETER OK. The landing. We left the rats.

MARJORIE Shit! They're all over the building. And they hate us.

MICHAEL Help her stand. It'll be faster around the landing. Peter. Take her left side.

PETER Marjorie hold the flashlights. Watch out! Shifting board. Don't step there. Grab her arms.

MARJORIE I'm gonna scream if my butt's fiery.

MICHAEL So scream.

PETER No screaming. The squatters. No screaming.

MICHAEL   One, two, lift.

MARJORIE   ARGHHHHH!!!

RALLY (*knocking*)   Open up! Open up!

MICHAEL   Focus. Keep going.

PETER   Can you make it down the steps?

MARJORIE   I think I can with you holding me.

RALLY   Open up!! Come on! Don't leave me out here.

MICHAEL   We're coming, Rally. Give us a minute.

MARJORIE   What a bitch. Fuck. I can do this. I can do this.

PETER   Got her? I'll get the door. Only eight steps left.

MICHAEL   Marjorie hold the light on the stairs. We don't wanna trip. That's how this mess happened.

RALLY   What the hell's going on? Open up!! Open up. I'm out here alone. Come on!!! They're coming.

MARJORIE   No, no, Michael. Don't leave me.

MICHAEL   I gotta help her. Ryder and his gang. Peter take over. I've got to let her in before they attack her.

RALLY   Michael. Please. They're here. (*screams*) MICHAEEELL!

Lights Dim

End of Act I

ACT TWO

Scene 1

Continuation of the previous scene. Michael and Rally on either side of the front door. Ryder joins Rally.

MICHAEL I'm opening the padlocks.

RYDER These are the other vigilantes.

RALLY I'm not talking to you.

Michael opens the door a crack.

MICHAEL Get away from the door, you! Rally, come here.

RYDER You breaking promises? We wanna talk. My word is my bond. I brought the vigilantes.

Peter and Marjorie join the others near the door.

PETER You're safe, Marjorie. Just stand and lean against the banister. I've got to run interference just in case.

RYDER We're coming in.

JUAN, FRANK, LOLITA We're coming in. Let us in. Yeah. Let us in.

RYDER Shut up, guys. I do the talking.

LOLITA You better talk to us. There's issues with this place.

RALLY Let me in Michael.

MICHAEL Just give Rally and me a minute.

RYDER   Talk to her in front of us. Don't slam the door in our faces.

JUAN   We come in good faith. Let us in. We claim squatter's hospitality

Michael grabs Rally, pulls her in, slams the door.

RALLY   Oww, Michael you hurt my arm pulling me like that.

RYDER   Throw your bodies against the door. Smash it, come on before they barricade it. Push! Crash it. Push!

MICHAEL   Come on. Come on! Help me with the padlocks.

FRANK   Door's heavy as a bitch

JUAN   Too fucking late. Dammit!

MICHAEL (*yells*)   Get off the premises. When you come again, bring the cake or don't bother.

LOLITA   This isn't war. Be adults! We're here to talk, you faggot!

MICHAEL   We're Squatters. And we know how things work. Occupy first. Negotiate never.

RYDER   Let's go. Come on. Follow me.

They leave.

PETER   Now what?

MARJORIE   I need to get the fuck out of here!

MICHAEL   You can't, until we come to an agreement with them.

PETER Agreement? Are you crazy?

RALLY We're their hostages if we don't. We can't just stay here and let them terrorize us.

MICHAEL I can't think.

PETER You're panicking.

MARJORIE Either we confront them, or lock up the building and leave. Then, they'll leave. I'm going anyway.

RALLY She's right. We confront them or leave with them.

MARJORIE The longer you wait, the weaker you look. We need to act. My leaving is an assertion.

RALLY How are you leaving?

MARJORIE With or without all of you.

RALLY But if we leave, it's like we're giving up.

MARJORIE I'm in pain. I'll tell them I'm leaving to get medication cause I have vaginal cramps.

MICHAEL The hell you are. Stupid excuse.

RALLY Better you say you broke your assbone.

MARJORIE Guys are creeped out by bloody vagina cramps. It will throw them off. One of you has to drive.

MICHAEL I forbid her to drive you anywhere.

MARJORIE (*screams*) ARGHHHHHH!!!!

PETER I can't take her anymore. She's the reason why we got fucked up, wasted time and didn't confront these lunatic bastards.

I'm boarding up the back door. They don't know I'm here. You don't need me.

RALLY They don't know Marjorie is here either.

MARJORIE I'm not here. In my mind I'm gone. If I had access to a phone, you'd never see me again.

MICHAEL I'll negotiate with them.

MARJORIE You don't have anything to bargain with. They have all the cards. They've blocked us from leaving.

MICHAEL We have conditions.

RALLY What?

MICHAEL They can't come inside.

RALLY Unless?

MICHAEL Never.

MARJORIE They're going to walk all over us, the moment they break in through the basement or get a ladder and—

MICHAEL Shut up. Let me think. Let me think.

RALLY We have to confront them. Cowards get beaten up.

MICHAEL (*sigh*) Then Marjorie comes with me.

MARJORIE To leave, right?

MICHAEL No one's leaving the building. You have good ideas. You're smarter than I am. Think of conditions.

RALLY You just insulted me. I'm smarter than she is.

MICHAEL   Not insulting you. I'm thinking about conditions.

On the other side of the stage, spotlight up. Lolita, Ryder and the others enter and confront Peter.

PETER   Stop it! STOP! You can't come in here. You can't come in. You have no rights, here. You can't—

Spotlight up opposite side of the stage on the others. Lights focus on speakers of both groups.

MICHAEL   Fuck. They broke in the back? SHIT. We're screwed.

RYDER   We can come in. Pre-thought rights. Hon, come on. Juan, Frank, stay and watch him. I'll call for you.

PETER   You're here unlawfully. We were here first.

RYDER   We're here to talk. But you don't wanna talk. You want jungle laws. You wanna fight? I said, you wanna fight?

MARJORIE   I told you I should have talked to them. You can't think on your feet cause you're flat footed.

Ryder and Lolita join Michael, Marjorie, Rally.

RYDER   Well all the devils are here.

MARJORIE   Lousy beginning, insulting us, whoever you are.

Peter gives something to Juan and Frank. They leave. Peter stands in the doorway watching Ryder and Lolita, their backs to him, then disappears.

LOLITA   The place has issues. Squatters need to beware.

MARJORIE   We're here first.

RYDER   We negotiate. The place is pre-thought squatted.

MICHAEL   You have anything in writing?

RALLY   What no cake? No bagels?

MICHAEL   Pre-thought? What are you Stalinist-capitalists? Pre thoughts? This isn't *1984*. It's acts that count. You are totally off square. We occupied the place. We thought it and DID it!

RYDER   Appoint someone else to speak. This guy is holding an economics class. AND WE DON'T WANNA HEAR IT!

MARJORIE   You mean poly-sci. I'll do the talking.

MICHAEL   Fuck you will. You said you're leaving.

MARJORIE   I'm feeling better. The pain is gone.

RALLY   Just wait. You'll be screaming and limping with daggers up your ass at night when it's the worst.

LOLITA   What happened? Fell through the floor? Ha, ha, ha, ha. A big issue. The floors can't be fixed. No repairs—

MARJORIE   Can I speak for everyone?

MICHAEL   Talk about it if you want.

RYDER   We don't wanna hear you. We negotiate or you won't stop us from kicking you out. Four on four. She's a black belt. You think you have pain now? Lolita will MAKE IT SO YOU WON'T FEEL FOR A YEAR. HA, HA, HA H

RYDER   Let's go upstairs and see what they fixed.

MICHAEL   Stay right there. You'll break your necks.

LOLITA   You're lying. What do you have up there?

RALLY Nothing you haven't seen.

MARJORIE You can't be who you say you are. Squatters believe in generosity. They don't bully or threaten. They have honor like the folks in number 17 with the big banner that says, "Occupied." They communicate. They listen. You say you're about negotiating but you're here to create chaos. You FAKEs.

LOLITA Who are you calling fakes? Look at you. You aren't for real. You're not dressed for squatting. Those shoes? No wonder you fell through the floor. You're your own wrecking crew in heels. Ah, ha, ha, ha.

RALLY And you're not the type to go the distance.

MICHAEL (*to Ryder*) Get away from the stairs.

RYDER Get your hands off me.

LOLITA You don't say what is for any of us. I say what is!

RALLY I've seen ten minutes of who you all are, and I know how to read your alphabet. A, B, C, Dumb.

MICHAEL If you're not part of the movement, you're spies working for the banks. We're not talking to you.

MARJORIE Prove who you are and we'll talk. Or get the fuck out and send others who can verify they're for real.

RYDER Same goes for you.

RALLY We're here. We showed up. We're doing the work. If you try to stop us, you'll see what you're up against.

MICHAEL For all we know, you've been hired to destroy the movement. Squatters have integrity. You don't know the meaning of the word. I can tell from your pale face.

RYDER   Empty insults. I'm going to SQUAT on this filthy floor and wait until you show us what you've done.

MICHAEL   We'll have a squatting contest (*sits next to him*). We're a part of the community. Who are you to say we're not? You stink of rat pee.

LOLITA   That floor is full of rat CRAP and God knows what else. We'll have to leave to clean up, Babe.

MARJORIE   So that's what you're doing? Going home to shower then coming back? Squatters stay and OC-CU-PY.

LOLITA   No working bathroom? You stink of rot and rat.

RALLY   We've been through worse.

RYDER   Eventually you have to leave. When you do, we'll pull you're shit down, unless we have agreements.

LOLITA   There's fines and violations on this building. Repairs gotta be done by a city contractor or they tear it down. In fact, the place is condemned and on the rolls to be demolished. It's coming up for a vote.

MARJORIE   Prove it.

RYDER   We don't have to prove it. It is. Ha, ha, ha, ha.

RALLY   You make no sense.

MICHAEL   If that's the way things are, then why are you interested? Why are you here?

RYDER   You have to fight for what you want. With the banks, with the city.

MARJORIE   But you aren't squatters. If you were, you would have been here before us and claimed the building.

LOLITA We were. They kicked us out.

MICHAEL   **MARJORIE**   **RALLY**
Who?   Who kicked you out?   But you came back. Who?

RYDER We came back because you're here. We came to tell you. But you won't listen.

MICHAEL So what you're saying is that the place is condemned and going to be demolished. And our repairs are gonna to be torn down. And we have to take your word for it?

RYDER Correct.

LOLITA The banks want this property. It's prime.

MARJORIE Prime? Completely wrecked inside and out. A trash heap. Dangerous. Rat infested. No banks are interested. You contradicted yourselves. Somebody's lying, and my friends at number 17 aren't liars.

LOLITA I mean the land. The land is prime.

RALLY You can't even put on a good fake. You're not here to prevent the demolition. You're here to make sure anyone who tries to stop it is kicked out or scared out. Someone sent you. They pay you. Who is it? Who?

MICHAEL Whoever it is, they're not the squatter's movement.

RALLY And you said you're the security for the area? Then you said someone else has the building? All bullshit.

LOLITA You wanna fight? Go ahead. See what happens. Come on!

RALLY I don't fight. I negotiate and compromise. But not with liars who can't spit straight.

MICHAEL   ENOUGH! You wanna squat on the floor? Doesn't matter. Peter! Peter! Come in here. Help me throw this punk out. We've wasted too much time with these assholes.

RYDER   Fucccckkk!! Get off me. (*He leaps up, pulls out a knife*) I carve up turkeys. Today's Thanksgiving.

LOLITA   Ryder, remember. We're supposed to come in peace.

RALLY	**MARJORIE**	**MICHAEL**
Ha, ha, ha.	Ha, ha, ha.	Ha, ha, ha.

Peter stands in the doorway.

PETER   What?

MICHAEL   Bring it. Show them you what peace is.

Peter leaves.

RALLY   Telling me to fight you is peace?

LOLITA   We've delivered the message. We're all leaving quietly. There's no reason for any of us to be here.

RYDER (yells)   Frank. Juan! Get in here! Frank! Juan! Now!

Peter returns with a shotgun.

PETER   Your boys aren't coming. I reinforced the door while you fronted. They're locked out. And you're locked in. Ya see this? Last time I used it, it worked. Maybe it does, maybe it doesn't. Shall I test it? I'll aim for your balls and see what kind of man you are. Give her the knife.

LOLITA   Let me have the knife Ryder. Easy with it.

MARJORIE   Ryder? Easy Ryder? Ah, ah ha, ha, ha. That's rich.

RYDER Shut the fuck up, cunt. Here, hon. Keep it handy.

PETER Big mistake, wanting to see if we made repairs. You should have stayed by the door to let your boys back in. They didn't look pleased when they saw me nailing the boards. But it was too late for them to do anything. In fact, they weren't even watching. They were in that back lot, smoking weed and doing uppers. I could tell they were slackers. Ha, ha, ha, ha.

RYDER If you boarded up the back, then we'll have to stay.

MICHAEL You go out the front.

LOLITA I'm leaving.

MARJORIE That's proof you're not squatters. You won't even ASK if you can stay. You should be negotiating to join us. Nada! Niente. Forget it. We take back our invitation.

RYDER That's your car out there?

PETER You touch the car, I can't be responsible for what'll happen with this rifle. It has a mind of its own.

RYDER It's her car, not yours.

PETER Communal property. You wanna stay, you're welcome. But we're tying you up until you tell us who hired you.

LOLITA Come on Ryder. We can't do anything without the others. Unlock the padlocks. I'm going.

RYDER You don't have to tie me up. I won't look around.

MICHAEL Yeah, you will. You wanna negotiate? What are you offering so I don't leave you in a dark corner to crap your pants? (*pause*) Lesson #1 about the rats you'll meet upstairs. It's an entire colony. Very clean. And, they take offense if you make a stink 'cause they have their own toilet. They know not to shit where they eat. They're smarter than you.

RYDER Hon, throw me the knife. THROW ME THE FUCKING KNIFE.

LOLITA I didn't come here to slice folks. We agreed to do what we had to, then leave.

RYDER Things have changed.

LOLITA If they don't leave when we leave, they get the consequences. I did what I had to.

Peter gives Michael the rifle, then leaves.

MICHAEL Ryder's staying, you're staying.

LOLITA Fuck him. I'm out. It's not my thing.

MARJORIE Thing? I wasn't aware of a thing. What thing? Easy Ryder, what thing?

RYDER She's full of shit.

Rally pulls Lolita's hair, struggles for the knife.

RALLY I'll just take that knife

LOLITA Fuck, no! ARGH! Stop. You're hurting me.

RALLY Didn't mean to kick you, but your hands are LETHAL. You're a BLACK BELLLTTT. I have to defend myself. Ryder, she gave me the knife easy. Easy, Ryder. Ha, Ha

MARJORIE You're lying about her being a black belt. Aren't you? Come on. Fess up.

RYDER She didn't defend herself so she wouldn't kill you.

MICHAEL   Neither of them has spoken one truthful word about anything since they got here.

RYDER   Let her go. She's useless to you. I'm staying.

RALLY   Both of you can't leave. If you do, you'll go back to your handlers.

LOLITA   What?

MARJORIE   Don't play coy. It's clear you're not activists. And if you aren't, you're trespassers. You threatened us. Ryder wants to stay? We'll oblige him and his partner. Upstairs. All the rats will be together.

LOLITA   I'm leaving.

RYDER   I'm staying, I want in.

Peter enters with rope from stage right.

PETER   Who wants to be tied up first? Welcome to Squattersville, the wild west.

MICHAEL   **PETER**   **RALLY**   **MARJORIE**
 Ha, ha, haha, ha, ha, ha, Good one.

MARJORIE   Tie prissy, first. She threatened us. Oh, but wait. Ryder threatened us, too. Hmmm. Geee.

LOLITA   Keep the knife. I won't take it from you. Open up the padlocks. I'M NOT PLAYING!!!

PETER   Rally, Marjorie, tie her up with this rope. Michael shoot if he interferes.

Marjorie and Rally tie up Lolita, roughly.

LOLITA AGRHH. Owww. Owww.

RALLY You probably work in a bank. Black belts have bruises. No bruises on YOUR arms. Liar, your thong's on fire.

LOLITA I'm an adept. I don't get bruises.

MARJORIE You're a bad liar who can't think on her feet. Sit!

Marjorie pushes her to the floor.

LOLITA ARGH!!!!! Bitch. Fucking bruiser.

MARJORIE Oh, sorry. Didn't mean to make you fall. And on your butt too. Ouch. Seeing you down there where you belong, I'm feeling no pain, ha, ha, ha!

RYDER I'm going in with you using my sweat equity.

MICHAEL Oh, right, yeah. You're joining us now? Fuck you.

PETER Give the rifle to Marjorie. Hands behind your back, Easy. Marjorie, shoot them if they fart.

Marjorie takes the rifle. Rally spots her. Peter goes to tie up Ryder with Michael.

MARJORIE You comfy? I want you to be comfy. Now, what's your name? Or is it just Easy Ryder's bitch?

LOLITA I don't have to tell you fuck.

MARJORIE I'm Marjorie after the film *Marjorie Morningstar.*

LOLITA Fuck your name.

RYDER I have information. You need to go in with me.

(Peter and Michael struggle to tie up Ryder.)

MICHAEL   The only place you're goin' is on the floor.

Michael pushes Ryder on the floor and slaps him.

RYDER   No! Don't, STOP! Oww! I have information. Information!

PETER   Help me turn him over, Michael. I have to secure his wrists.

Michael struggles to turn him over.

MICHAEL   You don't stop kicking, I'll slam your face into a pile of rat TURDS.

RYDER   Not the face. I just had crowns put in.

PETER   Those are some special knots he'll never get out of. Sit up! Rally you and Marjorie bring her over here. I'll check her knots.

MARJORIE   Get up.

LOLITA   I can't. I'm hurt.

MARJORIE   Where?

LOLITA   Where you pushed me.

RALLY   You're not hurt. Get up. You can walk.

PETER (*checks her wrists*)   Her knots are loose.

MICHAEL   What? Louder!

RYDER   I said I'll answer any questions you ask.

PETER   OK. They're secure. Rifle on them.

RYDER But what do I get in return?

MARJORIE Your freedom?

LOLITA What are you saying?	**RYDER** I'm making a deal, a deal.

MICHAEL You're going to give us answers. Then you go.

MARJORIE No answers? You can party with the rats.

PETER Who sent you?

(*Michael slaps Ryder*)

LOLITA This is kidnapping.

MARJORIE Only if we never release you. The way I see it, in a court of law, you attacked and threatened us.

RYDER It's a draw.

RALLY It's win win. Just tell us who you're working for.

LOLITA I don't know. He just rounded me up to help. He needed bodies. The other guys are from the block.

MICHAEL B.S.

Michael punches Ryder in the stomach.

RYDER OWWWWWWW.

MARJORIE You joined him for the fun of harassing people? NOPE!

PETER Agree.	**RALLY** Yeah, nope

MARJORIE Take them to the rats and darkness until they talk.

LOLITA The former owner of the building.

MICHAEL What?

LOLITA He owned the building. We're here as his agents.

RALLY Real Estate Agent provocateurs? Ha, ha, ha.

MARJORIE Upstairs into the black hole.

MICHAEL Marjorie, follow me. Rally, check to see if anyone's on the street. Let's go. Peter, him first. Upstairs.

Peter and Michael drag Ryder to his feet.

RYDER You're making a mistake.

MARJORIE The mistake was giving you a chance to redeem yourself. Punk.

RYDER ARGH! Don't push me.

MICHAEL If you don't go up there on your own, I knock you unconscious and we carry you. Careful. Don't leave the stairs or you'll fall through and kill yourselves.

They continue talking as they go up the stairs.

RYDER I'm going, I'm going.

MARJORIE You next. Go. Go! On the stairs. Near the walls.

LOLITA The former owner hired Ryder to watch the place and find out if anyone squatted.

MARJORIE What else?

LOLITA That's it. Shine the flashlight. I can't see.

MICHAEL He lost the building. The city took it over. The former owner is in jail.

LOLITA He's making arrangements with loan sharks for the money to buy it at auction.

MARJORIE Did the loan sharks give him the money?

LOLITA When the money's in his pockets, the loan sharks protect their interests. Don't tangle with them. They'll break your legs or throw you in Newtown Creek.

MARJORIE Guys. Wait. Get Rally. I can't go on the second landing. I'm creeped out. And my pain is back. (*yells*) Rally. Rally. Come here. Come here.

MICHAEL (*yells*) Rally. RALLY!

RALLY What?

MICHAEL Switch places with Marjorie. Take the rifle. Careful. Straight up around the landing.

MARJORIE I'm useless up there. My ass is killing me. I'll watch the door and think of a plan for them.

PETER (*from the top of the second floor landing*) Let's put him on the rat toilet. We'll tie her with him so they can't move. They roll around, they cover themselves in rat shit. Or fall down the stairs and break their asses. Their problem.

LOLITA I'll stand. I'm not sitting anywhere near that.

RYDER Don't waste your breath, Lolita.

RALLY Lolita? The spirit of Nabokov on a throne of rat shit.

PETER Rally, point the gun while I tie them together. Michael, help me tie them. Yeah. shine the flashlight.

Through this dialogue, Michael and Peter put the struggling Lolita and Ryder on the rat feces pile.

MICHAEL Down you go, next to "Hon."

LOLITA EWW Fucking bastard. Don't shine the light. No lights.

MICHAEL No? Oh. You gotta see this. It's two big SHIT piles. The rats always flush. Ah, ha, ha. Miss Nabokov.

LOLITA (*whimpers*) Why do you hate us? Why?

MICHAEL Breaking in, trespassing. I don't argue with liars.

RYDER We remember everything. You're in trouble, fuckers.

PETER No the trouble's just ending. Done.

LOLITA Leave us a flashlight?

RYDER You're supposed to be humane, honorable—

RALLY (*interrupts*) We're supposed to bend over and let you fuck us up the ass? Ha, ha, ha. After breaking in, you want us to be nice? When you're ready to talk, just call. Or send down a rat with a message. BBBBbye!

MICHAEL	PETER
Ah, ah, ha, ha.	Ha, ha, ha

They go downstairs, leaving Ryder and Lolita.

MICHAEL I always said that given the opportunity, women could be even more brutal than men.

MARJORIE Are you done with them? You have to drive me to the hospital. I need strong meds. My ass is killing me.

PETER Not the hospital. Just pick up aspirins and some supplies and come right back. Tying them up bought us some time. But we have to let them go. I'm checking the back door to see what's going on.

RALLY I think they should stay the night.

MARJORIE I'll stay the night if I have blankets and supplies and food and water and medication. Or I take the car, stock it with supplies, come back in the morning—

MICHAEL What happens if Ryder's gang comes?

MARJORIE No gang. They said those others were just some area bums they rounded up.

RALLY You can't believe them. They stay, we all stay.

MARJORIE They were desperate. They spilled their guts.

MICHAEL You're just saying that to get your way 'cause you wanna leave. No one goes until we agree what to do.

RALLY Let them stay upstairs.

MARJORIE If Peter tied them securely, they're going nowhere. I go to the hospital, get supplies and come back later tonight. You decide if you wanna let them go.

MICHAEL We're losing light. We can't get supplies. We need to stay in case we're raided.

MARJORIE OK. No hospital. Just supplies. I'll take the car. Rally, you come. The guys stay and guard the fortress.

RALLY The only way you go, is if I drive. You'll get into an accident if the pain worsens.

PETER No problem out back. The barricade hasn't been touched. Only problem is the place has one exit. One!

MICHAEL No one's going. I don't trust you two to come back together. You'll beg Rally to drop you at the hospital. She'll do it and then things will get super fucked up. If you come back tomorrow? It'll be over!!!

MARJORIE How dare you question my integrity! If I say I won't go to the hospital, I won't. And I won't beg Rally.

RALLY I'm not driving you there. So, get that out of your head. If we leave, we get stuff and come right back.

MICHAEL Whoever their bosses are, they know these fuckers are here. If you go, it's fewer bodies to fight back. They'll be a raid tonight. When we're most vulnerable. We'll have to use boards and hammers and wrenches—

PETER (interrupting) I'm checking if anyone's on the street. Michael, come with me just in case. I'm opening the door.

MICHAEL I don't hear anyone. You don't hear anyone do you?

PETER	**RALLY**	**MARJORIE**
No.	No one's out there.	You're paranoid.

MICHAEL So, everyone stays, and we wait.

MARJORIE This is crazy. You think the batteries in the flashlights are gonna last? Come on, Rally.

RALLY I drive. First, we go to a convenience store.

MICHAEL Peter. Get away from the door. No one's leaving. Peter, stop her.

MARJORIE Don't! (*yells*) I'm not in the mood for a war with you two. This Ryder guy messed with our heads and smashed our plans to stay. He frightened us and bullied you, especially, Michael. You've become a paranoid fuck. No water. No food. Dying batteries. No light. (*yells*) MORON! You wasted precious time. Rally and I could have been back with the stuff by now.

MICHAEL (*yells*) Shut the fuck up, bitch, before I come over there and make you shut up.

RALLY Can we just please calm down. Michael. You're stressed. You're ridiculous. Enough. Or I'm leaving and never coming back.

PETER The problem is what to do with them. The stress of kidnapping them is getting to us. We have to let them go. Have to. So, what if they run back to their boss?

MICHAEL They've seen what improvements we've made.

PETER So the fuck what? We can't go a day more without water. Food we can survive a few weeks. But if they raid us? We need bullets for the rifle to scare them. They got us off guard and now we're the ones all tied up and stuck and we can't move for shitting OUR pants. Don't you get it? They're the kings, sitting on their rat toilet controlling us. Everything turns on them.

MARJORIE Well said, Peter.

RALLY For fuck's sake Michael, we're going.

MICHAEL No one goes until I decide.

MARJORIE You've got fog brain and can't think 'cause you're dehydrated. Let me have the keys to the padlocks.

SILENCE

MARJORIE Oh, my God. You're so brain fucked by Ryder, you forgot you had the keys. Ha, ha, ha. Where are they?

RALLY Where are they, Michael? Michael?

PETER Are they in your back pocket? I'll get them—

MICHAEL GET AWAY FROM ME. You're not getting them.

PETER It's three against one, Michael.

MICHAEL Just try to take them from me. You wimp.

RALLY Now I know who you are. We can't even get through the first fucking day. We'll never make it through the real obstacles that will pile up for months and months. You are a weakling and a coward. How could I love someone. who's a tyrant, you HITLER!

MICHAEL I don't know. (yells) I DON'T KNOW. I—

MARJORIE Michael, it's not only on your head. We're a community. Three votes we leave, against one.

MICHAEL Not if I know you're wrong. I feel it in my bones. We need to stay. I feel something's gonna happen.

MARJORIE Go upstairs and check the rats and the darkness. Somebody. I can't.

PETER I'll go up.

RALLY Will you feel better if Peter guards them?

Rally feels around in Michael's pockets for keys.

MICHAEL No. All hands on deck. Someone has to help me with the front door and Peter on the back door. We work in teams. Rally, stop feeling me up. You're not getting the keys, you weasel.

MARJORIE Don't you see without the bullets, we have no way to frighten them? Then it's hand to hand combat. I'm useless without pain killers. (*pause*) And what if they bring guns? No cops. No help. They'll beat us and throw us into the street. If we're lucky.

PETER (voice over) (*from upstairs*) What are you doing? WHAT? STOP!!

MARJORIE Go see.

MICHAEL I'm gonna knock him unconscious if I go up there.

PETER (voice over) (*yelling*) Come up. Come up. You have the knife?

MARJORIE Something's going on. Go up. Hurry. I'll follow in a bit if my ass holds out.

MICHAEL Upstairs, Rally. Go, go, go, go.

Michael and Rally go upstairs.

LOLITA (voice over) (*screams*) Ahhhhh.you've set them off.

MICHAEL (on the stairs) We're coming, Peter.

LOLITA (voice over) ANOTHER ONE. OH MY GOD. TERRIFYING!!!

PETER (voice over) SHUT UP! STOP! MICHAEL!! Bring a board. Anything!

MARJORIE I smell something. Aghhh. My Ass. Agggh I'm coming.

Spotlight on the third floor, lit by the glow of a small fire which Peter is trying to put out. Ryder and Lolita are tied up nearby. Michael and Rally enter.

MICHAEL You did this motherfucker. The rat poop is on fire!

RYDER I'm not putting shit out!!! Ah, ha, ha, ha, HA, HA.

PETER Stomp it. Fuck! When you kick it you spread it, Rally.

RYDER The building needs to burn. BURN IT DOWN. BURN IT DOWN. HA, HA, HA, HA.

MICHAEL What do you know about this fucker? What?

PETER It's underneath the piles of TURDS. And sweepings and wood chips, newspaper. Stomp it. STOMP IT.

MICHAEL I'm trying for Christ's sake. Some accelerant is on there. It won't go out.

LOLITA Untie us. UNTIE US. THE RATS….RATS! THE FIRE!! FIRE!

RALLY You moved from the shit piles. Let me at ropes.

LOLITA Untie us. GET THE ROPES! I don't wanna burn alive.

RYDER Burn baby. COME ON BABY LIGHT MY FIRE HA, HA, HD, HA.

RALLY Hold still.

LOLITA Hurry, hurry.

PETER	**MICHAEL**
This board isn't good.	Use the flat edge.

RYDER You'll be guilty of felonious assault by fire. If you don't GET THESE FUCKIN ROPES OFF! You wanna kill us??

Smoke and flames increase.

MICHAEL STOMP IT!

PETER Get another board to help smash it.

LOLITA (screams) Ahgh! A rat just went over my foot.

RYDER Move! Move! Don't look at the rats.

RALLY Your wrists are free. Help me. Useless knife.

LOLITA Hurry up. Hurry. The smoke is making me sick.

MARJORIE JESUS H. CHRIST MY ASS IS KILLING ME.

MICHAEL Use this board Peter. Smash it. Don't let it spread.

PETER YOU USED AN ACCELERATE, YOU MOTHER FUCKER.

RYDER You think you're fucking tough? You have no idea. Bah, hah ha, ha bah, ha.

Marjorie enters.

MARJORIE I made it. *(coughing)* Wow. This place is gonna go up like tinder. Hurry. Put! It! Out!

RALLY HOLD STILL!

LOLITA A rat! Look! EWWWW!

RYDER Untie my ankles. TOO SLOW! I got it. I got it.

LOLITA A rat is right here looking at me. I'm gonna faint!!!!

RYDER I'm free. Here. Get up. Ignore the rats. Let's go.

MICHAEL (*yells*) It's not going out. You fuck. What? I'm going to shake it out of you.

MARJORIE Shit. I bet he used gasoline. Or some mixture.

RYDER (*yells*) BINGO. I SET THE NIGHT ON FIRE!!!

Ryder trips Michael who falls.

Oh, don't mind if I do.

MICHAEL AGHHH NOT…NOT AHHOOOO You bastard!

RYDER And what's a few kicks in the head between friends. Where are the keys. Ah, here.

Ryder rifles Michael's pockets.

PETER For that, you get a board in the face.

RYDER Not me. You!

Ryder fights Peter for the board, gets it, hits him.

Weak ass chump.

PETER ARGHHH

RYDER Ha, ha. How does it feel to be real? Got the keys.

LOLITA Come on Ryder. Down the stairs. Now.

MARJORIE Stop them. Rally. knock her down. Grab her legs.

RALLY Michael, are you OK? He got you good.

MARJORIE I'm stopping you.

Marjorie struggles to trip Lolita.

Down you go, Miss Nabokov.

RYDER I got ya…Lolita. Come on, come on, come on, come on.

RALLY Get up Michael. Get up.

Marjorie checks Peter as the fire still burns.

MARJORIE Peter, you OK? Wow. He got you in the face.

PETER NEVER MIND. The fire's spreading.

MARJORIE Everybody. Take off your jeans. They're heavy enough to smother the fire.

PETER No underwear. I'll use my T-shirt as underwear.

Peter ties his shirt around his middle, uses jeans.

MICHAEL He stomped my head. Dizzy. Rally take my jeans.

RALLY You can't stand up? Shit. OK. Pulling them off.

PETER The jeans are great. Use them there, where it spread.

MARJORIE Gimme his jeans, Rally. Use your leather jacket.

PETER Help me, Marjorie. Rally. Help. Now, over here!!

RALLY There goes my beautiful leather jacket.

MARJORIE (*at the flames*) Michael's jeans are smothering it!

PETER It's going out.

Scene switches to include front door downstairs. Simultaneous action downstairs and at the fire.

RYDER Fuckin' padlocks. These aren't the keys. There's a toolbox in the back. Need a hammer.

PETER Fire's almost out.

LOLITA Hurry up Ryder. (*fast*) Come on. Come on. Come on.

RALLY Just a few more areas need smothering.

MARJORIE I think it's out.

MICHAEL They're trying to leave. We have to stop them!

PETER Fire's out.

| **MARJORIE** | **RALLY** | **MICHAEL** |
| YEAH!!! | YAY | Hallelujah |

RYDER Fuckin' impossible. I have to pry open the boards.

LOLITA You said it would be easy. Hurry! I hear them screaming. The fire's out. You didn't put enough on.

RYDER We didn't expect four of them. Those women are bitches. ARGH….help me pull out this board.

LOLITA Just bash the padlocks with the hammer. Idiot!

RYDER OK. That's it. (*hammering*) Got one. Now the other.

LOLITA Hurry…uh oh. They're on the stairs!

MARJORIE You mother fuckers. You didn't care who burned alive.

Ryder gives the second padlock a smash; it opens.

RYDER Ah, ha, ha, ha. We're out of here… Come on Lolita…come on…come, come. I got the door. We're free!

Ryder opens the door to confront Sam who grabs him outside on the house stoop.

SAM Where are you going, CHAMP?

RYDER What? No…. What??? No…

SAM You were told not to be here. I'm gonna have my cop friends arrest you for trespassing.

RYDER Arrest the ones upstairs. They're the trespassers.

SAM Squatters are NOT trespassers. Something you people don't understand. THERE'S A DIFFERENCE. Adverse possession vs. unlawful entrance.

RYDER They set the place on fire. Go upstairs and look! Go!

HEDDY You're trespassing and if I hear you mention fire? You're the one that set it.

RYDER Fuck you. You have no proof. Trespassers. I saw them light it. I'm helping you out.

LOLITA They're the arsonists. We're saving the place.

SAM The fuck you are with the shit you pulled around here.

Marjorie is at the door. Sam holds a struggling Ryder.

MARJORIE Are you from the building that's occupied a few blocks over? Pewww. I smell like smoke. Putting out the fire.

SAM Looks like you succeeded. Time for arrests.

MARJORIE They started the fire with an accelerant.

HEDDY What's in your pocket?

SAM   See if he still has something on him.

RYDER   Fuck you will. Run. Lolita…run. Go, go, go, go.

Ryder breaks free, runs with Lolita. Heddy runs after them.

SAM (*yells*)   Let 'em go, Heddy. We know who they are.

MARJORIE   He set it. We're witnesses.

SAM   He's a hired arsonist. No one ever had any proof. Lots of insurance fires around here. Owners who walked away from tax liens and fines, destroyed their communities and created chaos. Rotten way to make money.

Rally joins Marjorie at the door.

RALLY   Hey! Who are you guys?

SAM   The Squatters' Project. We've been watching out for our movement. We make the rounds this time of day. He's bad news. Family connections, you know?

MARJORIE   You mean THE 5 family connections?

Michael and Peter join the others wearing their scorched jeans, shredded scorched tops.

MICHAEL   **PETER**
Hey.   Hey.

SAM   Wow. Looks like you've been through a war. So. What's the story with you guys? Four of you?

RALLY   We thought we were going to join you in the movement.

PETER   It's been fuckin' hard as a bitch.

MICHAEL We haven't even been here a day. Sun's going down, and we're losing our minds with this shit.

MARJORIE Real glad to see you. We need help. Ryder said he was one of you. It didn't add up.

SAM He's not. He's an agent provocateur out to wreck the movement. There's more like us patrolling the area for others like him.

MARJORIE Do you know my friend? Last name's Mullen.

SAM Jan? Our go-to-gal. She's the one you want to talk to if you're thinking of taking this building on.

RALLY We were so caught off guard. Ryder fucked with us.

MICHAEL Who is that guy? I wanna press charges.

MARJORIE He's connected. He's a world of trouble.

PETER We tied them up and brought them upstairs 'cause they attacked us. We played into his hands. Just what he wanted.to set a fire that couldn't be put out.

MARJORIE Except we did. Cause we're a community.

SAM I'll call a friend in the fire department to look at the char. They'll know. But at least now there's a material chain of evidence to charge Ryder.

HEDDY (*panting*). Whew. I got this off him. (*holds up vial*)

SAM Looks like Napalm. Easy, portable, unrecognizable, unless you know what you're doing.

MARJORIE Rally and I protested Dow Chemical about napalm in Viet Nam. And so it goes, from the Viet Nam War to civilian use. Scofflaw owners with family connections use napalm.

MICHAEL	**RALLY**	**PETER**
Totally fucked up.	WOW.	UNBELIEVABLE.

HEDDY We have to make our rounds. Are you gonna stay or go?

PETER I'm starving, dying of thirst, fucked up and I'm wondering if this shit is worth it.

HEDDY Ask that question 30 years from now when real estate in New York City is untouchable unless you're a millionaire or you're a part of a squatter community that is prospering unlike anything you can imagine.

MICHAEL Risking our lives for a wrecked building, rats, and hired arsonists torching it with us inside. MAN.

RALLY At least we got rid of the rats.

SAM	**PETER**	**RALLY**	**MICHAEL**
HA, HA.	Ha, ha, ha	HA.	HA, HA

MARJORIE There's still a lot up there. Oh. I get it. Ha, ha.

SAM Stop by Jan's. She has water and sandwiches, someone brought. And chocolate cake. Make sure you register. This is the last house under the movement. Hope you stay. You caught Ryder. None of us could.

HEDDY Nice to meet you. I'm Heddy. This is Sam.

SAM Maybe we'll see ya later at the building when we're done with our first rounds. Sorry you had an introduction to squatting by fire.

Everyone laughs. Sam and Heddy leave.

MARJORIE Oh, my God.

| **MICHAEL** | **PETER** | **RALLY** |
| What? | What? | What? |

MARJORIE My assbone doesn't hurt any more. It's a miracle.

MICHAEL Let's sit a minute on the stoop. I think it's safe.

MARJORIE You have something you want to tell us?

RALLY It makes sense. Ryder, I mean.

PETER I don't think any of this makes sense. I can just get a great job and make money, save for a house—

MARJORIE Not in Manhattan. Mortgage payments, inflation, tax increases keep you poor. You default, you become an asshole like these SCUMLORDS who walked away. You marry, have stress, get a divorce? Who gets the house? It becomes the spoils of war. Don't give up on the dream of community, dignity, unity, quality of life.

MICHAEL They're doing it. The Squatters' Project. They're working the plan. They're creating a haven. Anywhere else, it's not community building.

MARJORIE They have each other and they helped us today. Not out of obligation. Out of concern. We can be a part.

MICHAEL You really changed your tune.

RALLY Ha, ha, ha, ha. What got you onboard?

MARJORIE The Napalm. The war in the jungle is over. It's moved to civilian life. The little things we thought we'd always have access to are gone. Housing and food are harder to come by. No affordable place to live with owners napalming spaces and the city not building new ones. If corporations monetize real estate mortgages, it'll be over for us. It's economic warfare between the the haves and the have nots.

MICHAEL The middle class has to learn to fight back, not run.

MARJORIE Politicians keep voters in the dark. They commit crimes and pardon each other with impunity, like Ford pardoned Nixon last year. Now Republicans act like they're above the law and bully Democrats like Beame.

RALLY (*Pause*) If we had let Ryder terrorize us and run, we never would have met The Squatters' Project to feel we could be a part.

MICHAEL We'd be out of our house, burned to the ground.

MARJORIE It's not ours yet.

RALLY No. But after all we went through today?

MARJORIE Is that an answer somewhere in your question?

PETER Today was crazy wild. An adventure. Fun! (*pause*) I'm dying of thirst.

MICHAEL I want some chocolate cake, then a sandwich.

MARJORIE We have to lock up. Michael, you have the keys?

Rally checks Michael's pockets.

MICHAEL Stop feeling me up, Rally.

RALLY They're in his underwear. I don't think Ryder would have gone there. But I will ah, ha, ha, ha.

MICHAEL I wouldn't have let him. These padlocks are busted.

PETER Relax, there's more in my hidden stash.

The others go inside.

MARJORIE (*looks around*) The occupation has begun. (*pause*) My God. What have we gotten ourselves into? Ha, ha, ha. A squatter's paradise. Manhattan.

As Marjorie gets up and goes inside, lights dim.

THE END

MAXIMIZED SPACE

CHARACTERS

ROMY, freelance writer, separated, white female, lives in a rent-controlled apartment she inherited in the Village (20s)

DREE, Romy's BFF, single Black female, magazine journalist, mistress of Boone, who leases the UWS apartment where Dree lives (20s)

BILL, Dree's dorky, strange, hoarding neighbor who is actually undercover law enforcement and an investigator in the NYSAG's Office (30s)

MAC, Bill's attractive, ripped roommate, security guard, and undercover FBI agent working with Bill in a joint task force investigation (30s)

SAL, a thug who is the superintendent of ROMY'S apartment building in the Village (50s)

RUSSIAN FEMALE, Sal's boss with ties to the Russian mob (indeterminate age)

BOONE, Dree's cheating, wealthy lover from Texas who is married and travels for business (50s)

ELDERLY LADY, lives in Dree's building (80s)

YOUNG MAN – lives in Dree's building (20s)

MAN IN BLACK MASK #1, a freelance thug Sal hires for tough jobs

MAN IN BLACK MASK #2, a freelance thug Sal hires for tough jobs

BOB, a construction worker

SETTING

TIME: February 2020, through April 2020
PLACE: Manhattan, New York

The action moves between two very desirable neighborhoods
in Manhattan, the Village and the Upper West Side. Scenes
take place in and around Romy's rent-controlled apartment in
a building in the Village which has recently been purchased
by Luxurious Living, LLC And there are scenes in and
around Bill's rent-controlled apartment and the hallway and
elevator in a stable apartment building on the Upper West
Side where Bill, Mac and Dree live on the same floor.

ACT ONE

Scene 1

Evening, February 2020. Romy's rent-controlled Manhattan apartment. Romy prepares to take a relaxing bath with scented candles. As she turns on the water out comes a clump of huge roaches, not typical New York roaches. Romy battles the roaches.

ROMY Ahhhhhh! Ahhhh! Ahhhh! HORRIBLE. DISGUSTING. Oh my God! Oh my God. Girl, use the bathmat to mash them! DIE! DIE! I SMASH YOU! Ahhhhhh!

Romy turns off the water and continues to kill the scurrying insects.

MORE? What is happening? MORE! UGLY, FILTHY. LUXURIOUS LIVING! YOU NEGLIGENT, DO NOTHINGS. Uh, THEY STINK! I'M HEAVING! I'm going to vomit! THAT'S IT! I've had it! MY PHONE. WHERE'S MY PHONE?

Romy punches numbers into her phone.

SAL'S VOICE MAIL Not available. Leave a message.

ROMY Sal! They're coming out of the bathtub faucet this time. UNBELIEVABLE. GIGANTIC! ROACHES raised in a nuclear reactor. Extended families. I smash them. They ooze stinking grey ick. My bathroom smells of death. Their stink is worse than the rats you pulled out of the wall last month.

Romy paces furiously while ranting to Sal.

I'm choking, Sal! CHOKING! CHOKING. Luxurious Living is supposed spray the basement traps? Did they? Sal? PICK UP, SAL! SAL! You're supposed to be there for us 24/7.

SAL'S VOICE MAIL Mailbox is full.

ROMY Have I told you Sal, you and Luxurious living stink like roaches. Sal? (*pause*) You SUCK!

Scene 2

Lights up on Sal somewhere in the building as he talks to his boss a Russian accented female.

RUSSIAN FEMALE So, you got the shipment? All is OK?

SAL They've arrived. In the bathroom. She's crazy. Shrieking like a banshee.

RUSSIAN FEMALE Never mind crazy. Is she persuaded? She must be persuaded.

SAL I don't know. Yes. No. She's weird.

RUSSIAN FEMALE They are the biggest stinkers we could find. Did you put them where I told you?

SAL Of course. All of them.

RUSSIAN FEMALE Good. Good. Give me updates. Watch her movements. We have a big decision to make about her. We want to make sure she is easy, not hard. But we are prepared to go the distance where she is concerned.

SAL Copy. I'll watch her. Will speak to you later.
Sal clicks off as spotlight dims.

Spotlight rises on Romy in the living room.

ROMY   Stinks to hell. I can't stay here. I'll go to Dree's.

Romy clicks on her phone. Spotlight on Dree and Boone. They are on the sofa nuzzling and drinking prosecco. Dree answers.

DREE   Hey! My favorite best friend.

ROMY   Is Boone there? Are you busy?

DREE   What's going on?

ROMY   Can I come over?

DREE   Now? Just poured some prosecco. Boone's tickling my tender parts. (*sings*) We'll be going, "All night long, all night, all night, all night long, all night."

ROMY   Can we make it a threesome?

BOONE   Sure, darlin.' Why not? Come on over and rock with us.

DREE   No, no. Boone's flying out tomorrow.

ROMY   Too bad I'm not into threesomes. Charlie won't see me since we split. I can't stay with him. (*pause*) I can't get a hold of stupid Sal. He's not in and he's supposed to be.

DREE (*alarmed*)   Oh, no. Rats? Again?

ROMY   Can I please come over? You and Boone do a quickie. I'll kill the time before I get there.

DREE   Check the train schedules. There's construction.

ROMY I'll take a cab.

DREE Can you afford a cab?

ROMY I'll put it on my card.

BOONE (*snoring, then wakes*) Snrf, snrf. Wa, what? Kiss me, baby.

ROMY Afraid to stay here with THEM! I need sleep to go in early for work. Make it up to you.

BOONE Of course, darlin'. Take your time getting here. We're working out on our intimate lower levels, Ha, ha, ha.delicious lower levels.

**Lionel Richie (All Night Long)*

DREE Romy, dearest. Please make sure the "THEM" that's driving you out of your apartment doesn't share a ride with you uptown!

ROMY God. I never bite the hand that feeds me.

DREE It's not YOUR bite that worries me. The owner just evicted my neighbors for dog pee in the hallway. They're getting ridiculous.

ROMY I keep my apartment spotless. I don't get it.

DREE Boone thinks there's something weird going on in your situation. We'll talk about it when you get here…say an hour? See you in a bit.

Dree clicks off abruptly.

ROMY (*sighs ruefully*) Enjoy each other.

Spotlight down on Romy.

Scene 4

Spotlight up. It's two hours later, outside Dree's upper west side building. Bill presses the buzzer furiously.

BILL Come on buzz me in, will ya? OK. I'm sorry I forgot my key. Satisfied now?

MAC Asshole. I'm teaching you a lesson. You can just wait there. Let it sink in.

BILL Give me a break. I didn't take the key because you're there. Buzz me in. I got the info.

Romy sees Bill, runs up to him and hugs him.

ROMY Oh Bill. Thank God! I'm staying the night with Dree. Boone's in town but they're not answering. I left and came back. they're…

Door buzzes open. Bill and Romy go inside.

BILL Huh?

ROMY They're, ah. you know.

BILL Whatayoutalkin'about.

ROMY They started before I left. They've been at it over two hours—

BILL What?

ROMY You know. saying goodbye?

BILL They're not fucking in her apartment.

ROMY They have to be.

BILL No they don't.

ROMY They left?

BILL Yup.

ROMY I'll go up with you and try their door. They're probably back. Weird. No texts.

Spotlight dims, then rises. In the hallway in front of Dree's door.

ROMY Dree? Dree? Come on! Open up. Boone? Boone! *(pause)* Stop making love. It's me.

BILL You're going to tell a guy like BOONE to stop FUCKING? Ah, ha, ha, ha, ha.

ROMY Dree! Don't let me down like this.

BILL Enough with makin' a racket. They're not in.

ROMY You're sure?

BILL I rode down with them in the elevator.

ROMY Now, you tell me?

BILL You didn't ask for specifics.

ROMY Dree wouldn't do that to her BFF.

BILL Things change when a guy like Boone's in the picture.

ROMY *(ironic)* Thanks for reminding me about how lopsided men are.

BILL You shoulda told 'em you were comin'.

ROMY They knew. They were helping me out.

BILL Why? What's-a-matter?

ROMY Nothing. don't you have a key?

BILL No.

ROMY Don't you take care of the bird and those stupid ferrets when Dree visits Boone in Houston?

BILL I give keys back. Gotta pee. See ya

ROMY I'll just fucking wait. And rest. Need my neck pillow from my suitcase.

Romy opens her suitcase to get her pillow. A gigantic roach escapes. She races after it screaming.

ARGH! ARGGH! No! NOT HERE! You UGLY STINKING MONSTER. Stop! Not down the hallway. I got you! STOMP YOU. HAH! YOU'RE DEAD! UH. YOU STINK.

Bill opens his door. Looks down the hallway.

BILL Hey? What's goin' on?

ROMY HEY, Macarena. Ha, ha, ha, ha. Bill! Wanna dance?

BILL What are you doing?

Romy dances on top of the dead roach humming the song Macarena. Then she dances back to Bill who stands with the door open staring at her.

ROMY Trying out a new dance. The Bachata. Wanna dance Big Boy? Join me.

BILL I don't dance. And never in my hallway. Go to a club. Plenty of partners.

ROMY Can I use your bathroom.

Silence

ROMY Can I please use your bathroom? Dree's not back. Bill? Hello, Bill? Can I?

BILL Can you? No. You can't.

ROMY Why not?

BILL My wife left me.

ROMY You were married?

BILL Yeah, I was married. Don't insult me. She left. So… no.

ROMY Just one little pee. A teeny one.

BILL The Metropolitan Diner is open all night.

ROMY It's far. (*pause*) I promise to flush.

BILL No. My wife left me. I said, MY WIFE LEFT.

ROMY OK, OK. Calm down. What are you trying to say? For Christ sakes, say it!

BILL They went to a hotel.

ROMY What? How could they do this to me?

BILL Whatdaya mean how? Avoiding you. You're a pain.

ROMY Dree said she would be here. Something happened. She didn't call or text.

BILL   She had a suitcase. He was feelin' her up in the elevator. Right in front of me. Crazy. I had to look away.

ROMY   Christ! I should have pushed a threesome.

BILL   Boone takes sex very seriously. If you weren't goin' to have sex with the two of them, he probably got frustrated with you comin' and stopping his fun. Just go back to your apartment.

ROMY   I really have to pee, Bill. If I hold it, I get infections. Just for a sec.

BILL   I said, MY WIFE LEFT.

ROMY   What does that have to do with me peeing in the hallway, because I will.

BILL   No peeing in the hallway. It'll smell and Dree's ferrets will be blamed. No more BFF.

ROMY   I had tea. It runs through me. PLEEEEASSE.

BILL   Once you're in you're gonna wanna stay, and you can't!

ROMY   Nah. I stay at my own place—

BILL   That's why you're breaking down Dree's door?

ROMY   You're cruel not to let me come in and use your filthy, unwashed toilet.

BILL   I cleaned it. I CLEANED IT!

ROMY   Did you get down on the inside of the bowl with a sponge?

BILL   You women are nuts. We're done here.

ROMY   I'm taking off my thong. and peeing now.
ROMY starts to undress.

BILL   Stop. Stop! OK. But just to pee. Wait here.

Bill goes inside, closes the door in her face, gets a cloth, then opens the door.

BILL   Turn around. I have to put this on you.

Bill puts the blindfold securely on Romy.

ROMY   A blindfold? Is this fucking necessary?

Bill is a hoarder. Odd stuff, junk, newspapers, magazines, etc., are in piles everywhere.

He takes her elbow as he leads her.

BILL   I lead you to the bathroom. I, lead. You follow me. I lead.

ROMY   Get real. I'm taking this blindfold off.

BILL   Don't. STOP! My place, my toilet bowl, my rules. Respect me. Don't touch anything.

ROMY   Touch? I can't even see!

BILL   That's right. For my eyes only. I like my things as they are. Careful…step…step.

ROMY   Owww, ouch! OWWWW stubbed my toe. OWWW! Owww!

BILL   Careful! Don't go ahead of me! Wait. Wait! I lead you.

ROMY   It's unfit for human habitation, if you won't let me see.

BILL   You're so picky, go to the diner.

ROMY It's dribbling out of my crotch. I'll never make it. PLEASE!

BILL Women are wackos. Here's the door of the bathroom. And keep the blindfold on.

ROMY Thanks. If I went to the Metro in this cold, I'd be chafing yellow icicles.

As Romy closes the door, we see her take the blindfold off. Bill silently watches a large TV in the center of the room. Romy comes out without the blindfold.

BILL So, a 20-yard pass is how he did it!

ROMY Who's winning?

BILL What did ya do? I tole ya keep it on. Tole ya.

ROMY (*interrupts*) Was that a touchdown?

BILL You took it off? Where? Where's the blindfold?

ROMY Relax. I won't tell if you won't. I'm not staring at your junk heap, antique warehouse. It's so dark, I can't even see.

BILL Saving on my electric bill.

ROMY Male messiness is as ubiquitous as ear wax. Don't feel embarrassed.

BILL I don't! You! Go! Now!

Bill opens the door and waves his hand to sweep her out with the trash.

ROMY You don't have unwanted guests, do you?

BILL   Unwanted…you mean roaches? This is a Mitchell-Lama!

ROMY   The best. You prefer things your way.

BILL   Damn straight I like things my way. I don't want no woman making suggestions.

Romy opens a door to a bedroom and snoops around during the next section of dialogue.

ROMY   Hmmm. We have a way of doing that.

BILL   Get out of there! Don't! Close it. NOW!

ROMY   Doesn't Dree store some things in here?

BILL   She's got a bunch of stuff. I bring it out for her. I said CLOSE THE DOOR!

ROMY   I know. My guy friends freak if I see their filthy underwire piled on the floor.

BILL   Did you just insult me?

ROMY (*ironic*)   And what is this a, an antique?

Romy holds up an outrageous item.

BILL   Put that down, NOW!

ROMY   How many rooms are filled with stuff I'm not touching? See? Both hands raised.

BILL   Eight.

ROMY   What? You have three bedrooms?

BILL   And 2 1/2 baths.

ROMY Awesome.

BILL I make good use of the space.

ROMY You have a random order. The old radios and curios over here, and piles of old magazines over there and the Computer/TV right in the center. And this is out of order.

BILL LEAVE THAT WHERE IT IS. PUT IT BACK. It has to be there. Right there.

ROMY OK. I'm too OCD. I won't mess up your stuff.

BILL You have to leave! Out! Now!

Romy evades him.

ROMY Got anything to drink? Thirsty from peeing.

BILL You came! You peed! You leave!

ROMY What happened to good old-fashioned hospitality? Dree and Boone will be shocked when I tell them you're so horrible to me.

BILL Water. Then you go. I got stuff to do.

ROMY Isn't the game nearly over?

BILL I taped it. I'm analyzing the plays.

ROMY Gambling? (*pause*) Guys at work are gamblers. All they talk about. Huge pay offs. Mark is going PRO.

Bill is alerted. He shoves stuff on the sofa to the floor making a space where Romy can sit.

BILL (*very interested*) A professional, huh? Sit, sit, make yourself comfortable.

ROMY I don't want to keep you. I'll check on Dree.

Romy goes next door and comes back while Bill anxiously waits for her.

Fuck me.

BILL I tole ya. They're at a hotel where they're not bothered. Sit! Who's Mark?

ROMY Oh, I left my suitcase in the hallway.

BILL I'll get it. I'll get it. Go back inside.

Bill leaves. Romy gets comfortable on the sofa.

ROMY This place is fabulous. All it needs is a complete overhaul and an eviction.

Bill returns.

BILL I'll put your suitcase here.

ROMY You have any wine?

Bill grabs a half-full bottle of white wine from the refrigerator and shows her.

BILL There's this.

ROMY EWWW

BILL Wait. There is something else. You may like it.

Bill goes inside one of the bedrooms and returns with a bottle of red wine. In his absence Romy straightens a pile of magazines.

ROMY It's driving me crazy. Magazines have to be in neat piles.

BILL How about this? Hey. STOP. I tole you. You changed my stuff!. No Way. You got balls!

ROMY Sorry. I can't help myself. I'll mess it again.

BILL LEAVE IT! It has a special order. You're irrational!

ROMY Ah, a vintage wine. You MUST have a cooler.

Bill rearranges the magazines, messing them up like before.

BILL There. Now it's in order.

ROMY No straight edges to your order. Is your cooler in the bedroom?

BILL None of your business. You ask too many questions. Maybe you should leave.

ROMY You want to know about Mark, right?

Bill hands her the bottle and an old-fashioned opener. During the dialogue she opens the bottle.

BILL Just open it.

ROMY Is it your wife's cooler? (*pause, he doesn't answer*) Girlfriend's? (*pause*) Boyfriend's?

BILL Why you gotta be so nosy?

ROMY Are you rent stabilized?

BILL Are you going to pour or what?

ROMY These are beer glasses.

BILL Then drink it out of the bottle. All I got.

ROMY You're a mystery, Bill. Good wine but no wine glasses. So, you're rent stabilized?

BILL So Mark is a pro.

ROMY First you tell me about yourself, and if this magnificent apartment is stabilized.

BILL I don't talk about myself or my place.

ROMY Sip and savor good wine. Don't chug it.

BILL I'm thirsty. I'm chugging it!

ROMY You and your wife lived here?

BILL Are you deaf?

ROMY You finished it? You didn't even let it breathe.

BILL Wine makes me hungry.

Bill goes into the kitchen gets a bag of chips and brings them out without a serving bowl. He eats from the bag without offering Romy any. At times she pushes her hand in the bag and takes some.

ROMY Have you been here longer than thirty years?

BILL So, Mark makes enough money to go pro?

ROMY He's quitting his job next week.

BILL How much?

ROMY Can't. It's his personal business. I never share other people's business.

BILL We all do. He won't know.

ROMY I won't make public what's private. It matters if I tell you.

BILL Yeah. To me!

ROMY And me. And him.

BILL Why would you tell him you told me?

ROMY I wouldn't do it consciously. He may sense I told his secrets.

BILL He's not a mind reader, is he? Men are not mind readers. They're not smart like women to sense things. Men are stupid.

ROMY What a humble and flattering remark. I just may tell you—

BILL Tell me.

ROMY Nah…my conscience will bother me.

BILL Ha! No one has a conscience. Trump made it easy to get rid of consciences. Tell me.

ROMY You won't share how long you've lived here because of some weird reason. My conscience is my weird reason.

BILL Finish your wine and go.

ROMY Putting on my coat.

Romy gets her coat and grabs her suitcase, opens the door to exit.

BILL *(quietly)* I've lived here all my life.

Romy drops the suitcase and takes off her coat ready to deal information.

ROMY   So that means, you're rent stabilized.

BILL   How much does he make a week?

ROMY   Or rent controlled if your parents lived here and you inherited this spacious.

BILL   How much did he make in one month?

ROMY   I don't want to make you jealous.

BILL   I'm never jealous. Why would I be?

ROMY   It's human nature. Don't be disingenuous.

BILL   I'm very generous. What's wrong with being generous?

ROMY   Disingenuous. You know, duplicitous. dissembling. Twisting things

BILL   Nothing twisted. Old-fashioned curiosity. How much does Mr. Professional make?

ROMY   You'll want to do the same.

BILL   Yes, I want to do the same. Who wouldn't? Cash under the table? Don't be a conniver!

ROMY   You want me to make you into a criminal? Undeclared income? Ouch! My conscience.

BILL   Everybody cheats on their taxes. Tell your conscience to FLAKE OFF. (*pause*) You have a cruel streak. (*pause*) You're very sinister.

ROMY   What if you can't be like Mark?

BILL   Of course I can be like Mark.

ROMY Making $100,000?

BILL That's insane. It's not possible.

ROMY How do you know it's not possible?

BILL It can't be…unless, unless he's…

ROMY Is it possible to have a spacious 8-room, rent stabilized apartment in Manhattan for low rent? On the open market this place is worth millions! The rent could be $15,000 a month even if it's an unwashed DUMP full of JUNK.

BILL Unless he's a high roller and places a lot of big bets creating his own algorithms and computer codes, or bets Sports Books—

ROMY (*interrupts*) If it's rent stabilized, there are laws against kicking you out—

BILL (interrupts) You have proof? He's probably lying to get into your pants. He's probably a slob like the rest of us, living paycheck to paycheck.

ROMY How about the building?

BILL You can't get in here. There's a waiting list.

ROMY Why would I want to? It's too far uptown.

BILL It's a great building. Dree's here.

ROMY Dree's situation is different.

BILL Yeah. A Black woman, mistress of a married bigot, 25 years older. He travels for business so he can cheat with Dree on his wife, when he's in New York. And cheat with his wife on Dree when he's in Texas. It's his apartment. He dumps her, she's out on the street.

ROMY He's getting a divorce.

BILL Ha, ha, ha. Ha, ha, ha, ha

ROMY He proposed to her.

BILL You believe him? I should be asking if Dree believes him. (*pause*) She does. Poor thing.

ROMY (*angry*) Why would he lie?

BILL Men lie. Especially for sex. You don't know that? How old are you?

ROMY I think Boone loves Dree. I think Mark is truthful. And I think it might be nice to live here in your 8 room Manhattan apartment, but I have a place. And there's a downside if you're rent stabilized.

BILL No downside at all.

ROMY Oh, yes there is. (*pause*) Death. Death is the only way out.

BILL What?

ROMY You're forced to stay because of the cheap rent. At first when you move in it's YAYYYY! And then it hits you. I'm stuck. I can't leave. I'll die here.

Romy gets up and paces out her thoughts, obsessed.

BILL Come on. Folks go to Florida in the winter.

ROMY Another graveyard! Snowbirds never give up their rent stabilized apartments until they're DEAD. Then THE CURSE passes to their kids. And their kids have to decide. Should they stay until they die? Or do they choose freedom? Do they give up the apartment and LIVE!

BILL   How much does Mark really win? Tell me.

ROMY   Better job? More expensive apartment? Marriage? It's never good enough to leave rent stabilization. What if you get fired or get sick and go broke? You can't risk it. You are haunted by this hell you can NEVER LEAVE.

BILL   How does he do it?

ROMY (*frenzied*)   Death breathes down your neck, I'm herreeee. I'm your partnerrrrr. Rent stabilization is NOT great. It's a DEAD END! You're FUCKED!

BILL $100,00 over five years? That's nothing.

ROMY   If you have too much space, you are COMPELLED to fill every inch of it. And unless you hire a decorator, the place looks like it's a WRECK ROOM in the PSYCH ward of INSANE CHILDREN.

BILL   Go fuck yourself. You can't insult me.

Romy gets up and illustrates what she can do pointing to things to throw out.

ROMY   Hire me. I'll stay and clear the place. You'll be able to walk and breathe freely. You'll be a new man in a new apartment.

BILL   NOOO! NEVER! EVER EVER.NEVER!

Bill puts the chips, wine and glasses away during this section of dialogue. She follows him.

BILL   You realize he's playing you.

ROMY   He wouldn't play me.

BILL   Men play women all the time.

ROMY   You said women were smarter.

BILL   Some women. You're not one of them.

ROMY   You weasel! Why am I not smart? Because you got it out of me that he makes MORE than $100,000?

BILL   MORE? I'll be generous. In exchange I'll tell you my place is rent controlled.

ROMY   RENT-CONTROLLED? With this many rooms? Bill! You are amazing!

BILL (*ironic*)   What about it's being a "DEATH TRAP!"

ROMY   I might want to live here if it's DEADLIER than my place. Maximum space to DIE FOR!

BILL   You can't.

ROMY   If Mark can win more than $100,000 in one week, I can find a way to be in THIS building in YOUR apartment. How about we start now? I'll stay in one of your bedrooms.

BILL   In one week? Then he's with the Chinese gangs.

ROMY   Knew I shouldn't have told you.

BILL   You went public and could get your friend in trouble, just to find out about one of the finest rent controlled places in Manhattan. Rather pathetic. And desperate.

ROMY   Don't even begin to insult me, because if your decorations are any indication of what your interior mental landscape is like.

BILL How does he do it?

ROMY Can I stay the night?

BILL YOU brought in a mega roach.

ROMY Nah, not me…

BILL It's a stinking black spot on the carpet in the hallway.

ROMY It was on the bottom of my shoe.

BILL You crushed it <u>WITH</u> the bottom of your shoe doing your Bachata pee pee dance.

Romy goes to the kitchen to get a glass of water, drinks, calculating her response.

ROMY That was the only one.

BILL You can't stay. I can't risk it.

ROMY I won't open my suitcase. (*pause*) Please Bill. Don't make me beg.

BILL You have a place. I don't get it.

ROMY I'm afraid of going into my building this late. There's no doorman. They're doing construction. The elevator doesn't work. The lighting goes on and off. There's plastic sheeting. You can't see if someone is there to attack you. It's like that film where the guy is in an insane asylum and the patients sneak out from behind construction plastic walls.

BILL So my dumpy, crummy apartment is a palace by comparison? Ha, ha, ha.

ROMY Dree's not coming back. I'm homeless. You're interested. You want me to stay.

BILL You're not my type.

ROMY Would you like me to arrange to be your type?

Romy moves up to Bill and acts out a few types of celebrities or singers, i.e. Marilyn, Madonna

"I wanna be loved by you…" "Just like a virgin…touched for the very first time…"

BILL I'd like you to arrange a meeting with Mark.

ROMY He's very tight-lipped. You won't get anything out of him. We tried.

BILL But he lets your office know he's a big winner.

ROMY He's got a big mouth about winning. Not about how he does it.

BILL So in all his big winnings, he's a loser? He sucks.

ROMY I have a proposition to make.

BILL What?

ROMY I can run interference for you with Mark and set something up.

BILL For what?

ROMY A bed.

BILL Only I sleep in my bed. Too many diseases. My insurance deductible just went through the roof. I can't afford to catch anything from you!

ROMY You made it very clear I cannot charm you. But what about that lovely bedroom there?

BILL No, no, no. Off limits.

ROMY Then I'll sleep on this sofa in my coat, because your place is freezing.

BILL (interrupts) I haven't said, "yes."

ROMY But you will because I can find out anything from anyone, even Mark. I have skills.

BILL You're a woman. Figures. You wore me down. But only for tonight.

Romy grabs a bunch of tea towels from a pile from which Bill took one for her blindfold.

ROMY OK if I take these blindfolds for sheets? Oh. They're tea towels.

BILL So where is this going?

ROMY To Mark's doorstep. Then back to yours when I get the intelligence. I'll be your MATA HARI.

BILL Mata Hari. Ha, ha. I like that.

ROMY It's a deal. Good night. See you tomorrow morning.

BILL Lights off! Saving electricity. Sleep well.

Bill turns the lights off then leaves.

ROMY How do I get comfortable on this lumpy wreck of a sofa with tea towels for sheets? Sleep well? God help me.

As Romy settles in and falls asleep, a shadowy, ripped figure (Mac) enters. He moves silently through the dark room. He carries a blanket. He arranges the blanket on the sleeping Romy, waking her.

MAC   Blanket.

ROMY   Oh! You frightened me. *(pause)* Who are you?

MAC   It's clean. And warm.

Mac returns to the bedroom and quietly closes the door behind him.

ROMY   Very cute. Things are looking up.

Lights dim as Romy sleeps.

Lights up. Next morning, by the elevator. Romy waits impatiently, Dree enters.

ROMY Shit! I'm going to be late. What the fuck are you doing here?

DREE Where were you? I phoned and texted? You busted up Boone's and my whole evening.

ROMY Stop right there! You closed me out. You went to a hotel.

DREE What? We did not.

ROMY (interrupts) Bill saw you.

DREE He's a lunatic. We didn't go to a hotel. I can't leave Dickie and Weasel for more than five hours. They shred the carpet and destroy the furniture. I always ask Bill.

ROMY I call bullshit on you.

DREE Remember that time when Boone and I went overnight to my parents.

ROMY Such a liar. Bill said you had a suitcase. I waited at Bill's all night.

Dree pounds the elevator buttons.

DREE Elevator must be stuck on the top floor again. It's the old lady or the mother with her three kids and that slobbering Saint Bernard.

ROMY Don't change the subject.

DREE   You know Bill's doctor gives him magic mushrooms as an experimental therapy. And if he smokes weed, he overeats and hallucinates…Cristy told me. His word is unreliable.

ROMY   I didn't smell weed in his place.

DREE   He's also on Prozac, and he needs glasses.

ROMY   Snake! I was kicking your door down.

DREE   What time? We took a cab to your place to get you.

ROMY   You ditched me for your big, hot man. It's all about lover boy Boone. He made you so sex crazed, you forgot me. Left me afraid and alone staring into the abyss of homelessness.

The elevator door opens. An elderly lady is inside fixed near the door. She refuses to move.

ELDERLY LADY   Excuse me. Excuse me. No, no. Don't push me. I have to stay in the front with my walker to get out first. So just move over behind me. Get behind me so I'm in front. No, I said behind. Behind, behind me.

DREE   Not ALONE! You stayed with Bill. Did you try my door later? No! You took his word over mine. In your relationship with Charlie, it was obvious to Boone and me that you treated him like the bitch you are. The ink isn't dry on the separation papers and you're running after anything with THREE LEGS!

ROMY   Bruta! I ought to slap your face.

ELDERLY LADY   Please, No fighting. I don't like fighting. Stop. Stop it! Stop the elevator. Let me out. Let me get out. OUT! Don't, don't touch me.

The elderly lady ends up between Romy and Dree.

DREE Sorry Miss. But You're riding this bronco to the bottom with us. You can referee.

ROMY You're lucky she's here or I'd put you in the hospital SO YOU COULD PRESS CHARGES!

ELDERLY LADY No screaming. Heart palpitations. I can't breathe. Please. I'll give you all my money.

ROMY Keep your money lady. You're A WITNESS that I didn't BASH HER FACE IN.

DREE Go ahead. BASH me. TRY IT! BASH ME, Right here! On my CHIN!

ELDERLY LADY No. NoAh!! Ah.Ah, I'm fainting.

ROMY Go ahead. Smash me! Go ahead. Try it. Just try it, you weak sex slave.

DREE BULLSHIT. I can take you down any day.

Suddenly, the elderly lady becomes spry She takes her walker and uses it as a weapon.

ELDERLY LADY No one's taking anyone down. Back off you two cats. I got this. Back! Back!

Elevator door opens and we see a young man waiting.

ELDERLY LADY Oh, thank you. Thank you blessed virgin! Thank you, angel of mercy. Get away you witches or I'll take your eyes out with my walker. MOVE! MOVE! Watch out young man. They're like cats in heat. OUT! OUT!

The young man hesitates about going in. Dree and Romy are laughing. The Elderly lady gives one last shake of her walker at them then sprints away.

YOUNG MAN   What? What got into her? Are you both OK?

Dree and Romy laugh hysterically, ignoring him. He moves into a corner while they are wild with laughter.

DREE   Fear! The new arthritis cure!

ROMY   Ha, ha. oh my sides, my sides.

DREE   You see her jet outta here? Ha, ha. She won the Olympic 10 meter.

YOUNG MAN   There isn't a 10 meter. You're crazy. I'm taking the stairs.

He pounds the STOP button. The elevator jolts to a stop. The door opens, he quickly leaves.

ROMY (*hysterically laughs*)   There's another we scared away.

Romy sets the elevator to run again.

DREE (*laughing*)   We're elevator terrorists of the Upper West Side. That felt sooo good!!

ROMY   The hell with work. I'm late anyway. Let's take our act up and down each floor and see how the rest of the patients react.

DREE   Get a hold of yourself. I live here. You don't.

ROMY   I'm working on it.

DREE   I was right about you and Bill.

ROMY   Only if it was between him and Donald Trump.

DREE   Now I'm late.

The elevator doors open. They exit. Romy takes out her phone.

ROMY   I'm calling in sick. My head is pounding.

DREE (*upset*)   You have your phone? You couldn't text me?

ROMY   Something's wrong with it. It wasn't holding a charge. Or the chord is bad. I used a charger I found this morning, but it's only charging half strength. Walk with me.

DREE   So you never got my messages or calls?

ROMY   No. A complete blackout. What can I say? I'm sorry.

DREE   I am so pissed. Boone and I had a fight. He was upset we couldn't get a hold of you. We went down to your apartment.

ROMY   No fucking way.

DREE   Your super is a real shit. Make a complaint about him, if he's not union. He's not right in the head. (*pause*) Even if he is union, make a complaint.

ROMY   Awwww. So sweet! You came for me.

DREE   He didn't care if you were alive or dead.

ROMY   My other super loved me. The management changed and put in this bastard.

DREE   Your lights were on. You wouldn't answer the call button. He told us to fuck off. Boone was going to punch him out, but I pulled him away. We didn't want to make it worse for you.

ROMY   And I was banging on your door. And had to weasel my way into Bill's.

DREE   Boone came to Manhattan to relax, have fun. Now, he's steaming mad. He went back to Houston in a boil.

ROMY   I'm sorry about you and Boone.

DREE   I'll call you later. Get a new phone. I've been telling you to.

ROMY   Can't afford it. Let's go to the Metro. I'm dying for caffeine.

DREE   And don't forget to give that charger back to Bill. He hates sharing stuff.

ROMY   Bill? The Great Goblin of HOARDING?

DREE (*laughs*)   But some of that stuff is valuable.

ROMY   Not in two centuries. I stayed overnight. It's a trash pit in great need of garbage dumpsters.

DREE   Did you check what's in the boxes?

ROMY   The eyeballs of his X wife who left him? Ha, ha, ha, ha.

DREE   Divorced? Bill was never married.

ROMY   He said he's married. He wouldn't let me in at first because his wife left him.

DREE   I've seen him bring women over there. No wife. No one permanent.

ROMY   That son of a bitch lied to keep me out of his apartment. Something weird about him. I'll tell you what happened over breakfast.

DREE   No. I can't go in later than late.

ROMY   I need to talk to you about my apartment. You're my savior in this forbidden city.

DREE Ha, ha. Forbidding! The Forbidden City is in China. OK. You can buy me pancakes.

Lights dim as Romy and Dree walk

Scene 6

Lights up, later that day at Romy's place downtown. Romy stands in the hallway.

SAL Whataya doin' to me?

ROMY I live here.

SAL And I have to live here WITH YOU, you MENACE!

ROMY Not now. My head is pounding. Turn your loudspeaker down a few decibels. It's on DEAF.

SAL You're not funny…never funny. You're a MENACE!

ROMY You want to talk about a menace? Let's talk about this hellhole. I'm paying a high rent for a one bedroom with rats and Godzilla stink bugs and construction during sleeping hours.

SAL You're a vengeful, nasty, bitch. You sicked your friends on me at 11:00 pm, banging at the front door, buzzing everyone's doorbells.

ROMY Most of the residents moved out of this dump if they didn't accept the low offer the new owners made. There's a handful of people left in this rat hole, and I know they weren't in on a Saturday night in Manhattan when they drift in a 4 am. You are a prevaricator!

SAL You're not normal. No one uses big words like that because they want to make sense. You don't. Everyone heard your twisted friend and that Tex Mex guy screaming into the intercom.

ROMY The intercom worked?

SAL Everyone's complaining.

ROMY Who? All three people? No, actually two because I wasn't here.

SAL Don't try to be clever.

ROMY You're confusing mode with meaning. Why didn't you let my friends in?

SAL Mode? What? (*pause*) Why didn't I? The security of the building!

ROMY You're worried about security? People buzz at all hours. YOU LET THEM IN!

SAL You're getting revenge for the bugs. That happens again, I'm calling the cops.

ROMY The reasonable thing was to buzz them up. If I was dying, you would have been saving my life. What kind of scruffy person are you?

SAL I'm a person who wants his sleep and don't wanna be bothered by a bunch of nut jobs.

ROMY I know why you're like this! The owners told you to harass the hold outs, so they get frustrated and move out!

SAL You're crazy.

ROMY I hear landlords around the city are pushing renters out of their stabilized and controlled apartments. I did some checking. Luxurious Living has citations against it.

SAL I can't talk to you about the owners.

ROMY That's right because you've been hired to be their goon to scare us out! Since you've come, residents have left.

SAL   You better watch what you're saying to me. You're alone in this place. And anything could happen to you. Who would know about it?

ROMY   Is that a threat?

SAL   If anything should happen, you'd want my help.

ROMY   It's in the lease that you're not allowed into my apartment unless there's an emergency.

SAL   The definition of emergency has changed.

ROMY   What?

SAL   Water pipes breaking, stuff like that was the old definition, old owners.

ROMY   An emergency is an emergency.

SAL   We're doing construction. Anything can happen.

ROMY   According to city and state laws you have to give me notice unless there's an emergency.

SAL   All bets are off. It's CONSTRUCTION!

ROMY   The old super worked things out with me.

SAL   He's dead.

ROMY   When Luxurious Living took over, they stressed him so bad he had a heart attack.

SAL   We all gotta die sometime.

ROMY   If you do anything illegal or continue this harassment, I'll sue you personally.

SAL You have a lot of money for lawsuits? HA!

ROMY Speaking of lawsuits, where is the paperwork for the construction variances? I phoned and called the office eight times. Still nothing.

SAL I'll give it to you when it's ready.

ROMY You and your owners are going to be in big trouble with New York City and New York State.

SAL You don't know what you're talking about.

ROMY I'll get a lawyer for a class action against harassment. You can't force us out.

SAL I'm warning you! These people, this company, don't take kindly to troublemakers.

ROMY The company is the troublemaker. I want to see the variances, or you speak to our lawyer.

SAL Don't be stupid.

ROMY STUPID? I won't be insulted or threatened by the likes of you. What about the roaches?

SAL I called the exterminator.

ROMY Did he spray the traps in the basement?

SAL He's coming tomorrow.

ROMY I have to be there. When?

SAL Don't know. He freelances.

ROMY You have to tell me so someone can be there.

SAL   You can't have anyone present.

ROMY   He's a bonded exterminator, isn't he?

SAL   You can't be in your apartment. The stuff they use has chemicals that kill people. Takes a week for the poison to start to clear. Two weeks for it to be safe to enter. And, ya gotta take your plants out and cover everything. They're using bombs. Poison mist goes everywhere.

ROMY   Do you have these monsters, Sal?

SAL   Of course not! I'm clean! My apartment is brand new. The owners made sure that there are no cracks and everything's sealed.

ROMY   How convenient.

SAL   Good thing 'cause we got some real slobby renters still living here that bring roaches.

ROMY   I hear the residents who have bugs are the ones who didn't buy apartments to be renovated. In fact no one bought because the prices are ridiculous.

SAL   Whether you buy or rent, ya gotta get rid of the bugs. Bugs bring disease and filth. After Obama left the White House, they had a mess to clean up. Trump called a team of exterminators to get rid of the roaches, rats and dirt.

ROMY   The same team that exterminated roaches and mice at Trump's hotels? And at the Southern White House, Mar a Lago? Ha, ha, ha.

SAL   Humph! President Trump isn't Obama. He doesn't bring bugs and rats.

ROMY   Maybe I'll live with them, make them my pets.

SAL Prep your apartment. Go stay with a friend. You can hire me to clean up the dead roach piles. I'll do it for $200.00 an hour. It takes a day to clean up and another to air it out.

ROMY I don't want you or the exterminator in my apartment. I'm going jungle.

SAL What?

ROMY Screw your exterminator. I'll be Sheena, queen of this tenement jungle.

SAL Those bugs are everywhere. Take one more look. Then come down and tell me what ya wanna do, Sheena. I'll give ya an hour to decide 'cause I gotta make arrangements.

ROMY I decided. No exterminator. I'm taking care of this myself.

Romy leaves. Spotlight on Sal and Russian Female as they talk on their cell phones.

RUSSIAN FEMALE Why are you calling me? She should be out by now. Why are you letting her control you? She's just how you say, silly putty. You mold her to your will.

SAL I tried to get her out. It's not working.

RUSSIAN FEMALE It isn't working because you are weak. In this country you don't know how to persuade. In Russia we are very persuasive. No one tells us, "no." Because for us, "no" is not the right answer. Do plan B.

SAL (*pause*) I don't remember Plan B

RUSSIAN FEMALE You remember Plan A, don't you?

SAL Yeah. Very savvy. Very, very savvy.

RUSSIAN FEMALE   Plan B is NOT savvy.

SAL   Oh, yeah. No. Ah, wait… is that legal?

RUSSIAN FEMALE   Why you asking if it's legal? Of course, it's legal because we enforce it. Laws are broken 90% of the time, especially when no one is watching. You should be asking me how do we persuade her beyond her will?

SAL   OK. How do we persuade her beyond her will?

RUSSIAN FEMALE   You make what we want, her reality, whether she wants it or not.

Russian Female clicks off, leaving Sal confused, cut off as lights dim.

Scene 7

Lights rise on Romy's apartment as she phones Dree in her apartment.

ROMY I think I got them all. Thanks for all your help. Love you!

DREE Can't say it's my pleasure. Those things are BRAZILIAN RAINFOREST. They can do combat with tarantulas and army ants. Like I said, put one in a zip lock and take it to NYU's entomology lab. Get proof they are not New Yorkers and were shipped to you to get you out.

ROMY Can't. Legs twitching as they died in their bath of Raid.

DREE If Boone were here, he would catch one live.

ROMY How is he?

DREE Still mad.

ROMY Give it a week.

DREE He usually calls once a day. No calls. Nothing.

ROMY Call him.

DREE I'm too proud.

ROMY Not a time for pride. Call him tomorrow.

DREE Then you call those housing lawyers and catch a prehistoric creature and take it to NYU.

ROMY Will do it tomorrow. Sending you support strength.

DREE Sending it back. Call if you're lonely.

ROMY   I won't call you unless those creatures are eating me alive.

DREE   Don't forget to put your air conditioner on. They hate the cold.

They click off. Romy gets up and looks around the apartment.

ROMY   1:30 A.M. Yay! Not a roach in sight. Fuck you, Sal. Fuck you Luxurious Living. I'm still here! And I'm exhausted! Gotta crash.

Romy jumps into her bed, turns off her light by the nightstand. Romy snores. All is peace, quiet and darkness.

Scene 8

Moments later Romy's apartment door opens from the outside. A shadowy figure enters, closes the door. Crashing noises.

ROMY (*horror scream*) AiYYYEEEEEE.

There is the sound of a gunshot. Lights up. Romy stands pointing a gun at a hooded stranger, who stands with his back to the audience.

ROMY Get out. The next bullet has your name on it.

MAC But you don't know my name.

ROMY Thief! Robber! Rapist!

MAC Wait, wait, wait. We know each other. I'm just here to check…

ROMY I'm warning you…I'M A KILLER!!!

MAC LOOK! AT! ME!

Mac removes his hood and shakes out his hair then turns his face to the light for more visibility,

MAC You stayed with us last night. I put the blanket over you at Bill's place. It's really ah, both of our places.

ROMY Keep your hands raised.

MAC I'm the guy with the blanket. "It's clean and warm."

ROMY That's your place I stayed in?

MAC No. You stayed in Bill's place.

ROMY Bill's place, you're. what the fuck? Keep your hands raised.

MAC Can you please put the gun down.

ROMY Keep 'em up. Who are you?

MAC I'm Mac. You were sleeping on the sofa in Bill's apartment which he keeps like a doublewide dumpster. I put the blanket over you cause the living room is an icebox.

ROMY It was dark. You do look like that guy. He was ripped and cute. Ah, no…it's not you.

MAC You thought that guy was cute?

ROMY No. I mean he wasn't flabby and scruffy and doofy like Bill, and, and he was nice. He gave me a clean blanket.

MAC That's me. I work out and I'm very nice. Hey! You took my charger.

ROMY I gave it to Bill. Didn't he give it to you?

MAC Bill's a creep sometimes. I'm the real deal. In the flesh, I'm cute and ripped.

ROMY In the flesh you scared me to death. This protects me.

MAC Watch the gun! Don't wave it like that.

The gun goes off.

ROMY Ahhhhhh Oww. Son of a bitch! Charlie didn't say you could shoot yourself. AHHHH.

MAC You can't shoot yourself with blanks, unless you don't know what you're doing.

ROMY What did I do wrong? Owwww.

MAC You handled it like a toy gun. It's a prop gun. The old ones misfire.

Mac looks at her hand which is bleeding.

You sliced yourself. Apply pressure. You shouldn't wave around any loaded gun, even if it's an actor's prop.

ROMY Help! Bandages. Alcohol, bathroom cabinet top shelf.

They both go to the bathroom cabinet. Mac gets bandages, alcohol and wipes the wound.

ROMY OWWWW! That hurts. OWWWWW. Stop!

MAC Don't be a baby.

ROMY The gun's from my X who's a fight director. He handles theatrical weapons.

MAC Figures. (*pause*) This is still bleeding. You have any bacterial cream?

ROMY Up there.

Mac finds the cream and applies it. He puts on a bandage. Then, Mac examines the gun after they eventually move into the living room.

MAC Change the bandage, or it'll get infected. Your X should have said they misfire.

ROMY Very professional bandaging. Thanks.

MAC It's a Derringer. Used in poker scenes. See, it's rusted.

ROMY   He gave it to me after we split up.

MAC   Your X isn't smart. Dangerous to have anything that looks like a real gun and doesn't shoot live rounds.

ROMY   He wants me to be protected and safe.

MAC   It's not protection. If you were my girlfriend, I'd protect you in a different way.

ROMY   Why should you care?

MAC   You're alone. This building is a really scary place now it's under construction. You shouldn't be here. You should be in an apartment building that's normal.

ROMY   Why are you here?

MAC   I'm security.

ROMY   Security? I don't remember you.

MAC   Recently hired. Kids were stealing the copper wiring faster than we could put it in. I work the night shift, officially over at 5:00 am. What's your name?

ROMY   Romy. It's on the door unless that bastard Sal took it off. You know, you broke in.

MAC (*shows her*)   Keys. I have access to every apartment.

ROMY   Yeah, but my apartment is occupied. You're guilty of breaking and entering.

MAC   I buzzed. I don't think the buzzer is working. And I knocked for five minutes.

ROMY   The buzzer sometimes works. But I can hear knocking. You didn't knock.

MAC Five minutes I knocked. I heard noises and a scream. I have to check out stuff like that.

ROMY I screamed?

MAC Do you go to a psychiatrist for night terrors?

ROMY I don't scream.

MAC I heard ungodly noises coming from this apartment, then a scream.

ROMY Hmmm. I do snore, but only when I'm stressed.

MAC Pretend to snore. I'll tell you if that's what I heard.

ROMY Don't insult me! (*pause*) I can't hear myself snore. Charlie said I'd be a great monster in a horror movie. Supposed to go to a doctor, but Charlie's gone, so I didn't go. Saving money.

MAC You weren't snoring when I put the blanket on you.

ROMY I felt safe. Bill's place is a wreck, but I felt secure for the first time in a long while.

MAC Ha, ha, ha. Before or after the blanket?

ROMY Well, ahmmm.

MAC Sleep apnea. So, you're continuing to stay here without a roommate or boyfriend?

ROMY Yes.

MAC You want to know what I think?

ROMY Not really. Are you Bill's roommate?

MAC   No! I'm neat.

ROMY   Then why were you there?

MAC   We have an arrangement.

ROMY   So. You're gay.

MAC   No. Are you interested? I'm available.

ROMY   I mean. ah, what do you think?

MAC   About what?

ROMY   What were you saying?

MAC   You shouldn't be here. Being alone stresses you so bad you have night terrors. You scream in your sleep and you're not aware of any of this. You're a danger to yourself, especially with sleep apnea.

ROMY   Charlie never said I screamed.

MAC   You probably didn't scream because he was with you. Before the scream what I heard scared me. Indescribable. Growling and howling like wolves or cougars, animals fighting.

ROMY (*embarrassed*)   All right, all right… that's enough.

MAC (*laying it on*)   I was pounding. There was snarling and ferocious, vicious, animal noises. I broke in to stop whatever horrible attack was going on here.

ROMY (*humiliated*)   OK. You made your point.

MAC   You shouldn't be here alone. Your sleep apnea is off the charts. You have to get that checked. Sleep apnea affects your heart. You could have a heart attack and not know it.

ROMY (*annoyed*) If I have a heart attack, I'll know it.

MAC No you won't. You'll be dead. You're too young to be the heart attack type. But with severe apnea, your heart stops. Someone must wake you, or your heart stops forever.

ROMY I'll get a dog and train him to bark.

MAC Whatever. If you didn't hear me knocking and pounding, you're not going to hear a dog.

A mammoth roach races across the living room, followed by others. Mac tries to get each of them, fails, succeeds, fails. Simultaneously Romy screams.

ROMY (*screams*) AHHHHHHH! AHHHHH! EWWWW NOOOOO!

MAC Got one. Another! Take that. Where are they coming from? Oh, sorry I broke your broom. But I got 'em. Nope. There's the granddaddy. You son-of-a-bitch. Broom's not totally useless. Those are some ugly motherfuckers! Whew! They stink. I'll clean this.

ROMY Uh…I feel woozy. Maybe I'm not the queen of the jungle I thought I was.

MAC Put your head between your legs.

ROMY I'm fine.

Romy collapses. Mac catches her and puts her on the sofa. Then he gets her some water. She drinks as he cleans up the roach mess.

MAC You're probably dehydrated.

ROMY If you're security where's your uniform?

MAC Logo's under my hoodie. When you shot that Derringer at point blank range, and I wasn't hit, I knew it was a prop. But you still scared the shit out of me. Good thing I restrained myself from using this.

Mac pulls out a gun.

MAC   A Glock. It's licensed.

ROMY   Oh God.

MAC   You're lucky I'm trained to shoot only when someone has to go down. But that Derringer misfiring could have taken out my eye. Give it back to Charlie or give it to me.

ROMY   I need it.

MAC   It's not going to protect you. You're alone. You've got a sickness that can kill you. Anything can go wrong. No one is here to help you. Oh, yeah, you can't have pets in the building. New regulations. So, forget the dog.

ROMY   I'll work things out.

MAC   Go to a doctor. Charlie's right. You sound like monsters!

ROMY *(edgy)*   My snoring didn't end me and Charlie.

MAC   If that was the reason, Charlie's an idiot. Get a roommate or lover. Let the company spray. Looks like you have a bad infestation.

ROMY   I think the bugs are under control. I'm persistent.

MAC   You're foolish. They're only going to get worse when mating season rolls around.

ROMY *(angry)*   Enough! I'm handling it!

MAC   You're doing a lousy job. Let the company experts do it.

ROMY And be out of here for two weeks or more? Get real!

MAC If you don't stop this infestation, rejecting their exterminator, they WILL evict you.

ROMY They can't. I'm rent-controlled

MAC After they kick you out, I'll be paperwork mind games to make you give up if you sue. Lawyer letters. Court dates, delays and cancellations. Save yourself the stress and money.

ROMY I'm seeing a housing attorney today.

MAC Why go through this stinking hell? Let them take care of the bugs or just move out.

ROMY Bullseye. Now you said it. It's why you came during the night. To frighten me away.

MAC I'm doing my job. Now, I stayed too long.

ROMY Meet me later for coffee.

MAC Working.

ROMY Then after later.

MAC Not allowed. Company policy.

ROMY They won't know.

MAC They know everything.

ROMY Not if I run into you at Bill's.

MAC You won't. I just dropped in to see him 'cause I was uptown.

ROMY   What if I want to see you again? Do I have to scream at 4 am to get your attention?

MAC   Now that I know you have night terrors, I'll let you fight it out in your sleep. IF you stay. (*pause*) Don't!

ROMY   Whatever.

MAC   Let them exterminate. Stay in a hotel. Take them to small claims court. They pay your hotel bills for as long as you're out of here.

ROMY   If I leave, they won't let me come back.

MAC   They'll let you back in. You just may not want to BE here. (*pause*) Didn't they make an offer for you to vacate?

ROMY   It's not enough of an offer to find an equivalent apartment. No one took their offers. I'd have to leave the city. I've lived here for 8 years at very low rent. New York City is my home.

MAC   You don't want trouble. Do what they want or get ready for the fight of your life. Start small. Move up to the City Housing Department, then the Attorney General.

ROMY   I'll think about it.

MAC   Do more than think. Decide. (*pause*) You repeat any of what I've said, I'll call you a liar.

ROMY   I hear ya and I fear ya, ha, ha, ha.

MAC   Stay safe (*pause*) Romy.

Mac leaves

ROMY   Kinda dreamy in an ironic way. (*pause*) Hmmm. Wait. Where? It must be here.

Romy searches on the sofa and backtracks where she last saw the gun.

It was here. You took it? You tricked me? Then, you're one of them. You can't be trusted, either. Fuck you, Mac. Fuck you, Sal. Fuck you Luxurious Living. I'm staying.

Romy storms back to bed, thinks.

You're gonna give my Derringer back! (*pause*) But how? How do I get in touch with you?

Romy goes to turn the lamp by her beside off then considers, keeps it on, lies back on the pillow.

No more sleeping in the dark!

Lights dim.

End of Act I

ACT TWO

Scene 1

Lights up. March 2020. Romy is in her apartment on the phone with Dree in her apartment.

DREE Glad you finally talked to the city housing lawyer. You're doing better than me. I'm going nowhere with Boone. (*yawns*) Exhausted. A minute more. Any return of the bugs or Mac?

ROMY No Mac, no bugs. I hope I never see him again. Like I said. He's with Sal and the company. They're housing terrorists.

DREE Too bad. Why are all cute guys evil?

ROMY I'm worried. The building is deadly quiet. It's like everyone left.

DREE The company frightened them away. That's what happened.

ROMY I'm so stupid. They offered to move my stuff out and move it back once they renovated.

DREE You know they're liars. You can't trust any of them.

ROMY The lawyer said they can't evict me, if I pay my rent. Wait. I hear someone in the hall. It may be Mac. Hope not. Call ya later.

Romy opens the door to Sal.

SAL You still here?

ROMY That guy Mac who you sent, didn't scare me. I pulled a gun on him. Same goes for you if you break in. I've taken care of the roaches.

SAL Yeah? What are you gonna do about the pandemic?

ROMY What?

SAL The pandemic. All the smart folks in the building left. You're the only holdout.

ROMY What do you mean?

SAL That China virus is spreading. They're gonna do like what they did in cities in Italy. Shut everything down. I got cousins there.

ROMY That's kissy, huggy Italy, not here.

SAL Shut up and listen to me for once. The company bought out everybody. Spent a lot of money to do it. Now, they can renovate in peace and charge fifteen times the amount when they're done (*pause*) And then there's you. The only holdout.

ROMY I've been listening to the news. It's just the flu. One day it'll be gone like a miracle.

SAL What news are you listening to? DiBlasio and Cuomo pulled off a quarantine now they closed the education system. The city's essential workers are on the job, regardless.

ROMY (*interrupts*) Oh, my God. You're serious.

SAL It's a pandemic. Yeah, I'm serious. Pack your bags. Go stay with relatives.

ROMY I'm...oh God. (*pause*) But I can't leave.

SAL New York has millions of people squished together. No sane person is staying. They don't wanna get it. Folks will die in the streets. Die like rats.

ROMY Sal, I inherited this place after taking care of my dying aunt. It didn't come to me easy. I had to fight for it. (*pause*) No bugs or thugs or COVID gets me out. I assert my rights to stay.

SAL This lab-engineered virus was made in China. And it doesn't give a damn about your inheritance or your rights. It's contagious as hell. You stay, you're gonna get it and there's no one who's gonna give a damn you're dying 'cause it's every man for himself.

ROMY You're being an alarmist.

SAL I'm being nice. Look. I never liked you or that other one, what's his name…

ROMY Charlie.

SAL Whatever. But this is no place to be alone in a plague where they close off the city.

ROMY Same old Sal. Your fear tactics won't work.

SAL Make no mistake. This building will be shut down. They won't keep the electric and heat on. Get out while you can.

ROMY They can't shut things down. I LIVE HERE!

SAL You're the only one. You're alone. Who cares about you? You call 311. I have no lights, no heat. So what? It's better than being dead. Don't believe me? Go on YouTube.in Italy…

ROMY You lied before. You're lying now.

SAL And you're too stupid to breathe. Have a good night. Don't let the bed bugs bite. Ha, ha.

Romy slams the door behind him as he walks out. Romy phones Dree

ROMY I'm totally freaked.

DREE What did Mac say?

ROMY I can't believe it. But what if it's true?

DREE What's true?

ROMY You listening to the news?

DREE Not since Boone left. We used to watch it to see his boy Trump. I can't bear to now.

ROMY The pandemic in Italy. COVID-19. They closed the schools. Work places next. People are leaving the city in droves. You haven't heard?

DREE I'm not feeling well. I have a cold. I haven't been out. I'm so upset about Boone. Heard nothing from him. Just playing music and catching up on Netflix films and TV shows.

ROMY Sal said look on YouTube to see what happened in Italy. The same is happening here.

DREE They can't close. Think about the logistics. Too difficult. (*pause*) Don't worry.

ROMY What if Boone doesn't come back from Texas? What if he stays with his wife?

DREE He takes care of me. He always takes care of me

ROMY In a city full of disease? This is different.

DREE Why are you so negative? Boone is a gentleman. It's his apartment. I'm the only asset that comes with it that matters to him. Ha! He's not giving me up.

ROMY The city has the plague. People with money evacuate. They cut all ties with contagion.

DREE He's not like that. I know him. He likes his comforts when he travels. He hates hotels. *(pause)* Anyway, I've been here for over a year. I have squatter's rights.

ROMY You hope. Like I hope I won't lose my mind, being alone in this creepy building.

DREE We have to help each other.

ROMY Live together?

DREE The owners won't allow it. I won't even ask

ROMY They don't have to know

DREE Boone will be pissed. He's mad at you, anyway

ROMY Forget it. I'll survive. I always do

DREE I know there's room here and stuff, but it's…and I don't feel well.

ROMY Forget it. I don't want you to jeopardize your relationship with Boone.

DREE Things can't be as bad as you say. They can't!

ROMY Sal says people will be dying in the streets like in China.

DREE That's ridiculous. And I heard it's just the old people. Look. it's not the 1700s when the flu was a killer…when there was no medicine. Sal is a fucking torturer. And now you're torturing me. Just stop it, please.

ROMY You haven't heard a word I said.

DREE I choose to ignore you. Ha, ha, ha. *(pause)* I don't feel safe without Boone.

ROMY Can't wait until this blows over by Easter, like Trump said. I hate him, but I feel comforted by Fox News. They aren't so dire. Anyway, when it's over, I'll press harassment charges against Sal.

DREE That's the spirit. We've got each other's back, right, BFF?

ROMY Es verdad. Hasta la vista, Chica.

They click off. Lights dim.

Scene 2

One month later, April 2020. Sal is on the phone with his boss, spotlights on each.

SAL She's impossible. She should 'a left by now. No electricity. No water. No elevator. No heat. No gas. Just COVID. I tried everything.

RUSSIAN FEMALE Not everything.

SAL No, no. I'm not doin' that. Not on her.

RUSSIAN FEMALE You have to. With the lockdown, they're not allowing construction unless there's no one in the building. Get her out. Now is the perfect time. NOW!

SAL I heard different. No construction at all.

RUSSIAN FEMALE That BS is for public consumption. The entire New York City skyline is being changed as we speak. Cuomo and D.B. have many emergencies. No time to check construction sites. As long as there's no one occupying a building, no one knows. Right? (*silence*) I said, right?

SAL I don't know. I don't…look, I don't know about it. I don't like it. There'll be fallout.

RUSSIAN FEMALE Don't be a weak ass just because she's a female. You wouldn't give me lip if it was a guy. Maybe you're a dead spider and I wipe out your web?

SAL Don't fuck with me. For the record, I tape record our conversations and give them to a vicious, hairy bastard with an overbite. (*pause*) Gimme a week. Then I'll let you know.

RUSSIAN FEMALE You've got three days. If she's not out, say goodbye to your $10,000 a month apartment and welcome to the world of unemployment. I'll see to it you won't get a job anywhere in this city. You'll be able to work in Alaska.

SAL Yeah, yeah.

Yeah, yeah

RUSSIAN FEMALE   JUST DO IT!

They click off their phones. Spotlights dim.

Lights up. Evening, three days later. ROMY is in bed with heavy sweaters and a coat. A flashlight shines as a night light. There are sounds of pounding and demolition. Dust falls from the ceiling. Romy jumps out of bed and screams and pumps her fist up at the ceiling.

ROMY   I'm here, you sons of bitches! STOP! Or I'll beat your heads in! Hawk! Cough. uh, so much dust…plaster…cough, cough falling on me! Argh! Light in the hallway so they can work at all hours, but they cut me off? Fucking outrageous! No one would put up with this. No one! SO! WHY! DO! I?? FOR AN APARTMENT THAT'S 600 SQUARE FEET? FUCK ME! But this is MY INHERITANCE. A little slice of Manhattan? RENT CONTROLLED. So few RENT CONTROLLED LEFT. It's "My Own Private Idaho." Fuck you, Charlie. You abandon me to thug Sal and this Luxurious Living NIGHTMARE? (*pause*) THIS IS NO! WAY! TO LIVE! How do people do it? No heat. No power. In the subways. Homeless families. SO THE RICH COLLECT THEIR GROUND RENTS? Luxurious Living, you're SCUM! You want me outta here? (*pause*) There's nowhere to go. Dree's got COVID. No one's taking care of her! What if she dies? What if I get it? I'll die alone in this horrid apartment choking on dust clouds and COVID. Stop panicking! STOP! Breatheeeee! Think! Legally this place is yours. You leave, you lose it. Years of lawsuits. You'll never be able to afford Manhattan again. My phone is dying. I don't care. I need music! MUSIC! 'Cause I'M STAYING, YOU BITCHES!

Romy clicks on her phone and sings along with Katy Perry's' "ROAR"

"You held me down, but I got up and now I'm brushing off the dust. You hear my voice. you know that sound. Like thunder, I just shake the ground. I see it now, la, la. I'VE HAD ENOUGH! I've

got the eye of the tiger, a fighter, dancing through the fire. I'm a champion, now. hear me ROAR!"

The apartment door shatters off its hinges kicked in by one man in black followed by another.

MAN IN BLACK IN GAS MASK #1   Hey! Hey! Stop dancing! Nut case! CRAZY!

Romy gets a bat by the door and starts to swing it, defending herself.

ROMY   Get out! I'll bash your head in. Get out

MAN IN BLACK IN GAS MASK #2   You're too weak to bash anyone's head in. Gimme that bat. Take her phone.

Man in Black #2 wrestles with Romy for the bat and takes it.

MAN IN BLACK #1   Gimme the phone or I bash your face in.

ROMY   I'll kick you in the balls. I know Kung Fu. Ha!

Romy defends herself, looking like she knows martial arts.

MAN IN BLACK #2   Watch her! Watch OUT! Just use the stuff.

MAN IN BLACK #1   I don't wanna use too much.

Romy takes the flashlight on the night stand and clicks it off. The stage is in darkness.

ROMY   No flashlight. No more light now, bitches Take that!
We hear voices, grunts and sounds of pain.

MAN IN BLACK #2   Awwww. Aooowww. She got me. Use it! Use it!

MAN IN BLACK #1   I can't see shit. Where are you? Come to papa, pretty one. Come, come!

We hear wrestling sounds and grunts.

MAN IN BLACK #2   I gotta a flashlight. Here!

Man in Black #2 turns the light on. Romy is in the corner behind the sofa in attack position.

MAN IN BLACK #1   There.

ROMY   When I'm done with you, your balls will be hanging by a thread.

MAN IN BLACK #2   Use the stuff or give it to me.

Both rush Romy. Then stop in their tracks.

ROMY   I have COVID. *(spits)*   TAKE MY SPIT YOU BITCHES. *(spits)* You touch me, TAKE MY COVID! ARGH! *(spits)*   TEWWWW

Both men stay the six feet distance away as she spits at them.

MAN IN BLACK #1   I'm not goin' near her.

ROMY *(sings)*   "Come and get YOUR LOVE." Ha, ha, ha. I wanna kiss you! Come on! GIMME A HUG, KISSSY KISS, just like the Italians who died in Italy. KISS *(spits)* KISS!

MAN IN BLACK #2   What are we afraid of? We've got masks on. Come on. Do it! Do it! You can't? Throw me the bottle.

ROMY   I'm looking at a dead man. I've got the plague, and I just gave it to you. It's in my spit. It's all over you both. Welcome to respirators and strokes and heart attacks. *(maniacal)* Ha, ha.

Man in Black #2 rushes her. Romy fights and spits and kicks.

MAN IN BLACK #2   Help me. Hold her. Hold her! Get her legs!
Man in Black #1 douses a tissue with liquid from the bottle and covers the struggling Romy's mouth and nose.

MAN IN BLACK #1   Think you're a tiger? Ah, ha, ha. You're just a weak-ass girl.

ROMY   Awk Argh. Ohhh.

Romy collapses on the ground.

MAN IN BLACK #2   Christ. I shoulda brought my tazer.

MAN IN BLACK #1   Yeah. End this shit quick.

MAN IN BLACK #2   You think she has COVID?

MAN IN BLACK #1   Let's wash up and throw her in the shower before we take her.

Lights dim.

Scene 4

An indeterminate amount of time later. Lights up on Romy lying on a white sofa in a well-appointed, apartment. Mac, in a chair, wears a mask.

ROMY Agh. Oh. I'm heaving bile. Ewwww. My head's squeezed in a vise. AGH!

MAC Don't throw up on the rug. No. Watch! Watch! It's a white carpet.

Mac gets a bowl, a glass of water and a towel as Romy heaves her guts on the carpet.

MAC Christ. Here. Throw up in this. Wipe yourself. DRINK.

ROMY You!!! What? Ehh, owww. EWW Water is good.

Romy drinks as Mac wipes up the mess.

MAC There was a body reported in the fire escape stairwell. I brought you here.

ROMY Water never tasted so good. SLEDGEHAMMERS UP HERE. Where am I? Oh, OH, this is a renovation. I bet no prehistoric stink roaches are here either.

MAC Don't get comfortable. Your stay is temporary. What happened?

ROMY Nope. Can't even sit up. You're spinning in circles. I have to heave. Zennnn. Zennn.

Romy throws up on the carpet.

MAC The bowl! The bowl! Christ. You missed.

ROMY If it's any consolation, heaving doesn't help.

Mac throws down another towel after he dumps vinegar on the carpet and cleans it.

MAC You do it again, you clean it.

ROMY Like this is fun? EWW. I'm ack ARGH.

MAC Drink the water. You were at the top of the stairwell about to roll down and break your head open. I saved you from.

ROMY (*interrupts*) YUCK! Nothing like tasting throw up.

MAC Hydrate.

ROMY My mouth tastes like pee.uh.

MAC Who knows what pee tastes like.

ROMY Don't ask.

MAC Doing better. Haven't thrown up for a minute.

ROMY Just wait. Uh. Can't sit up. Where's gravity?

MAC Get your mind off how you feel. (*pause*) What's the last thing you remember.

ROMY Uh. I'm a champion. You're gonna hear me roar.

MAC (*laughs*) Champion?

ROMY I'm too sick to sing it for you. Uh. EWWW.

MAC Have some of this. It's ginger, good for dizziness, nausea.

ROMY Sit down you're rockin' the boat. Waves crashing. Uhh worse than a hangover.

MAC I warned you, ah, forgot your name.

ROMY Just call me idiot.

MAC Ah.Homey.Romy…that's it.

ROMY Wait. oh…I was dancing to Katy Perry.

MAC Do you remember what I told you?

ROMY Hey! You have my gun! I need it when I go back to my apartment.

MAC Gun's busted. I threw it away.

ROMY It was valuable. You owe me a Derringer.

MAC No gun. You don't know how to use it.

ROMY I'd use it against myself. How hard is that? Just point at my head and shoot.

MAC You're not suicidal, are you?

ROMY I was hit over the head. I fell. My body's a pustule ready to explode. There's the plague and your boss is freezing me out. I have no paycheck. No work. But it's my apartment. I inherited it. I have a right to be there. I'm! NOT! LEAVING!

MAC You're desperate.

ROMY You have NO IDEA! I'll die before I give it up. So fucking tell your boss that he's going to have to kill me to get me out. Just messing with my heat and electricity and plumbing isn't enough! Especially with COVID out there and, and. Oh! I can sit up.

Romy stands.

I'm standing! Have to get my phone, charge it.

MAC You can't go to your apartment.

ROMY What???

MAC Someone broke in trashed it and stole stuff.

ROMY I don't believe you.

MAC Do you remember anything?

ROMY All I remember was dancing and singing and I have to go there.

Romy paces slowly.

MAC Don't make me show you. It'll be one more horrible thing you go through. You're emotionally very unstable now and suicidal.

ROMY Fuck suicidal. I'm furious. You're security? You let this happen! I'm going to sue Luxurious Living and you, you, YOU INCOMPETENT SON OF A BITCH!

Romy heads for the door. Mac blocks her path.

MAC Hold on. Let me tell you, then you decide. There's food here. I can make you something.

ROMY Food? (*pause*) I haven't had anything to eat.it feels like days.

MAC There's snacks. Sit while I get it ready. SAL has COVID. I had to call 911 and take him to the hospital. He's on a respirator.

ROMY   Crap! The place is booby trapped with COVID.

MAC   Speaking of COVID, there's masks over there. You should put one on.

ROMY   Are you sick? Oh. yeah…wear a mask to protect the other person.

MAC   I was with Sal when my security team called about a body in the hallway.

ROMY (*breaks down crying*)   I can't handle this.I, I, I'm going upstairs to see what's what's.

MAC   You're a tornado. Stop for a moment. Here.

Mac hands her her phone.

ROMY   My phone?

MAC   I saved the one thing that looked like it was worth something. While you were unconscious, I went to your apartment. I'm sorry. but, there's no living there now.

ROMY   You charged it? So kind. I lost my charger. My phone's my only lifeline.

MAC   It took a long time to charge. There's cheese and crackers on the kitchen counter. They're high end. There's wine? Or you still feel worse than a hangover?

ROMY   My phone. Thank you. I am grateful. Wine? OK.

MAC   It's a Pinot Noir. Just carry the bowl and stay away from the white rug.

Romy gets a cracker and cheese and pours herself some wine. Mac gets a glass for himself. Romy sits at the counter, checks messages, and texts. Mac nervously paces at times.

ROMY I got a lot of messages. Dree.

MAC (interrupts) Who's Dree?

ROMY My friend.

MAC Can you stop texting a minute.

ROMY I'm telling her what happened. Why?

MAC To talk about you. What you're gonna do.

ROMY Go back upstairs after I have this great wine.

MAC Your apartment isn't functioning.

ROMY I know that. I choose to be there.

MAC You're not safe. It's dangerous.

ROMY I'm with building security. I'm safer than I was, except I need another gun.

MAC Put the phone down. Can you please listen?

ROMY You have something worse to tell me than what I know they want me out and probably sent some fucks to trash my place assholes!

MAC I can't provide your personal security. The company owns my ass. They started renovations on the apartment which isn't yours anymore.

ROMY That's crazy. I'm NOT out of there.

MAC You don't want to get into it with them. Your place was invaded and you didn't stop it. And you didn't report it.

ROMY You bastard! Somebody either hit me over the head or, or tried to throw me down the stairs and and forced me out of there. I didn't leave of my own free will.

MAC And you can't remember shit. So what good is a police report?

ROMY For now, I can't remember. It's coming back.

MAC It's a losing battle against these people.

ROMY How come you know so much about "these" people? What people? Who? You sound like Sal.

MAC Sal's barely alive. We don't know how he got COVID

ROMY What? They intentionally infected him?

MAC Does anyone know how somebody gets it? People breathing on him or he got it from a polluted surface. It's microscopic. It lingers for hours. Sal wasn't the cleanest guy.

ROMY You brought me to this place to infect me?

MAC No one who's been here had COVID. That I know.

ROMY My stuff THAT THEY TRASHED.

MAC Maybe drug addicts living in the subways. They're robbing apartments for stuff to sell. A lot have COVID. They're turning people away from hospitals. Maybe your stuff is contaminated and when they carried you, breathed on you.

ROMY Oh, God.no, no.

MAC Try to remember. What happened?

ROMY I can't remember. It's a blank. I need coffee.

MAC I'll make it. But we have no milk.

Mac makes coffee.

Do you remember a break in.

ROMY Bug eyes. I remember bug eyes. Traumatic. I don't wanna remember. I want to rest. I need coffee.

MAC Coming up. *(pause)* we can go upstairs see what's left of your stuff.

ROMY I don't want my stuff if it's polluted with COVID.

MAC Take your clothes and wash them. Use this apartment while you decide what to do. Construction and the owners use the place at times. I'll speak to the company on your behalf so you can stay here for a while. But you have to pay.

ROMY And I go back to my place once I clean it up.

MAC That's over.

ROMY Then this is an illegal eviction!

MAC It's, it's not an eviction. It's a lot of factors. COVID, the invasion.

ROMY That's beyond my control. No security, drug addicts busted down my door and smashed and grabbed? This is against the law. I'll fight this.

MAC How? With what? In the middle of a plague that has no known cure and is killing people, with the number of dead rising? We're quarantined. Look at the latest YouTube post by the governor about rising infections. Deaths. DEATHS! There's no room in hospital morgues. They've got refrigerator trucks piled up with bodies. Thousands have left the city. It's a ghost town. Do you really think your situation is a priority? They're dropping dead in the subways. We don't know the half of it. De Blasio wants it quiet 'cause it's out of control. It's CHAOS.

Mac hands her a mug of coffee.

ROMY It's…it can't be THAT bad.

MAC You were in a time warp. And in denial, like everyone. No one cares about you 'cause you're alive. At least if you were dead, they'd tag your toe and refrigerate your corpse.

ROMY Shut Up! I can't hear this.

MAC You have to make decisions about your life.

ROMY I want to see my apartment. I have to stay there.

MAC We'll go. You won't believe me otherwise. Mask up.

ROMY I heard masks don't work.

MAC This is a new virus. There's no immunity. Diseases don't belong to a political party.

Mac hands her an N95 mask.

The walls are demolished. Nothing is sterilized like here. There's probably COVD. The elevator isn't working. We'll take the stairs. What's wrong?

ROMY I.I.I. (*pause*) I want to believe you.

MAC Some things have to be seen to be believed.

ROMY My life. Everything that means anything to me.

MAC In the twinkling of an eye. A plague.

ROMY Disappeared.

MAC If you face reality, you'll know what to do.

ROMY I already know. Sue you bastards.

MAC Where are you going stay while you sue?

ROMY My apartment.

MAC It doesn't exist.

ROMY In a sleeping bag with a pile of rubble for my mattress.

MAC That's giving it order. There's no solid floor.

ROMY I'll sleep in the hallway.

MAC Either way, you'll be arrested for trespassing.

ROMY I'll stay here tonight and go to court tomorrow.

MAC Don't you get it? NO COURTS ARE BEING HELD. The COUNTRY IS IN LOCKDOWN. They are setting up remote courts on Zoom. It's like live video in real time. Until this plague ends, what are you going to do? What if it's months and months?

ROMY Dree texted me. The cold she had blew up into COVID. I can't stay with her. I'll go to a fleabag hotel or a shelter.

MAC Shelters are full of COVID. Poor bastards. Twice damned and they're being told there's nowhere else to go.

ROMY Coffee's clearing my confusion. I have to stay here.

MAC Unless I intervene, you won't be able to.

ROMY You have no reason to lie to me, but I just can't believe you!

MAC You WON'T believe me. Let's look at what is. Don't cling to what was. You can't argue with facts.

ROMY I can't bare it.

MAC Stay here where it's warm. You have the use of the facilities. I'll speak to the company and see what can be arranged.

ROMY I never was so alone in all my life.

MAC You're not so alone. I'm trying to help you.

ROMY You're with them.

MAC If I was in your shoes, traumatized by drug addicts, stuff stolen, lost my apartment, I'd think the same. But I'd know when someone was helping me, someone who was taking a risk.

ROMY You're not at risk.

MAC You don't know anything about me. Am I not asking that you live in a premiere apartment while you figure out what to do? That's against policy.

ROMY Don't they have to provide somewhere else for me to live since they illegally EVICTED ME?

MAC They didn't evict you.

ROMY What do you call taking my apartment and destroying it?

MAC A renovation. It was uninhabitable. Door bashed in, place wrecked, stuff gone. You were brought here for safety. They didn't have to do that.

ROMY What about laws?

MAC Laws? To catch the people that smashed and grabbed? Cops are working with EMT now. It's all about COVID. I told you there are no in person judges, no courts.

ROMY You said courts on Zoom.

MAC Try making a complaint in this city. No one is at the helm. De Blasio can barely put one foot in front of the other. It's a highly contagious plague. No one is prepared. Not hospitals, not shelters. Only essential workers for EMT, sanitation and grocery stores are out there. The only one who is doing anything is Cuomo and the legislature is PISSED to give him absolute executive power in an emergency to save us. And meanwhile Trump is saying it'll go away, like a miracle. He's made it a New York plague. No one in the South will get it. The Red States shouldn't fear. COVID is a Blue State Democrat. Don't wear a mask. It's the "IN" thing in the South and red states.

ROMY Oh my God, I'm an asshole. I didn't want to believe COVID was so dangerous.

MAC With this chaos do you really think anyone cares about you? You have to save yourself and get the fuck outta Dodge. Leave Manhattan. Go where it's safe.

ROMY Where is that?

MAC Anywhere with low COVID numbers. We're the death capital of the United States.

ROMY I can't go anywhere else.

MAC You have relatives. Go stay with them.

ROMY I don't know.

MAC I'll try to work something out. You better get something lined up. Unless you come up with $10,000 a month.

ROMY The place isn't worth $10,000 a month.

MAC You're not in a position to say what something is worth. Finish your coffee. I'll make the call.

Mac leaves. Romy facetimes Dree. A screen shows the conversation.

ROMY Oh, my God. You look horrible. Are you drinking water with lemon and taking zinc?

DREE (*raspy*) I tried. I can barely breathe. (*between gasps*) Still have a fever, I'm dying (*coughs*) argh! Argh! ARGH! And no one cares.

ROMY I care. You have to call 911.

DREE (*gasping*) I don't want to die in the hospital.

ROMY Have you heard from Boone?

DREE (*raspy*) ARGH! ARGH! I got an eviction notice. It's over.

ROMY WHAT!

DREE He planned the eviction for months. Didn't pay the rent. When he came to visit, it was one last fuck fest and, and (*coughs*) ARGH! ARGH! ARGH!

ROMY Shhh. Calm your mind. Please, please, Dree. Go to the hospital.

DREE A Black female, alone? They're turning people away. I won't come home alive. ARGH! ARGH! ARGH!

ROMY I'll go with you. Dree, Dree. I'm coming up there.

DREE (*crying*) Don't. You'll get sick. I want to die. I hope I die. ARGH! (coughing) We were planning our wedding.

ROMY God damned red neck son-of-a-bitch. Nothing good comes out of the Houston oil industry.

DREE COVID. It's everywhere in my apartment. I'm a death trap. Boone was smart to cut me loose. I'm just a fucking loser.

ROMY Stop it. If you need anything have Bill help.

Mac comes back.

ROMY I have to go. Elderberry tea and fresh lemon. It will cut the crap in your chest. Love you. AND I, CARE! Call you later.

MAC What's going on with your friend?

ROMY Sick with COVID. And. she's being evicted.

MAC Nothing to be done. The real estate industry controls the city. Cuomo put a moratorium on evictions. Some places are fighting it. She may be out on the streets.

ROMY Her lover didn't renew the lease, didn't pay the rent. He was stringing her along. Bastard red neck, racist, misogynist.

MAC This may be an opportunity for you two to live together.

ROMY If she lives. Her place is full of COVID. She won't go to the hospital to die.

MAC Do you believe me, now? You're lucky the company lets you stay here.

ROMY Am I? For how long?

MAC I got you a month for $6000.

ROMY $6000? I don't have $6000. How am I going to live? I need, food.

MAC $1400 a week for the utilities and space.

ROMY What about construction and owners coming here?

MAC They can't use it. You're here, you have to pay. That's the offer. Or take the money you have and leave the city.

ROMY I can't just pick up and go on quick notice.

MAC You don't pay, I call the cops. Trespassing.

ROMY The cops are busy with COVID.

MAC These people have friends on the city police force. If you're arrested, you'll be in a crowded jail. COVID is on a killing spree there.

ROMY You're a prick. What happened to the guy that put the blanket over me in Bill's apartment when I was cold? Whatever happened to the guy that bandaged the gunshot wound.

MAC The way it is. Cough up the money or you're out.

ROMY I'm remembering, now. You're not a hard ass. It's what I liked about you.

MAC Don't fool yourself. And don't like me.

ROMY You were flattered that I thought you were cute, way back when I shot you, or rather shot myself. Seems so long ago.

MAC It doesn't matter.

ROMY You're still attracted to me. You're better than being a goon for your criminal bosses.

MAC What if I am? These people are still these people. Everyone's out for themselves.

ROMY It's THAT attitude that landed us in this horrible plague with ERs turning people away to die alone. (*pause*) I think I know a place to stay.

MAC No.

ROMY Bill will let me sleep on the couch again.

MAC The place is a hell hole.

ROMY But it's across from Dree.

MAC She's being evicted.

ROMY And Bill, as crazy as he is, has a kind heart.

MAC There's no room.

ROMY You're living in a space with three bedrooms and a huge kitchen and dining room and two baths and.

MAC (*interrupts*) It's a garbage dump. We're under restrictions with COVID. They want to kick Bill out.

ROMY Away from this glass castle of fur-lined shit, you have a heart. These people make you a fuck.

MAC Whatever. (*pause*) They said some clothing and items were put in garbage bags in the basement.

ROMY Who? Did they have COVID?

MAC Wash anything you take.

ROMY They're only things I have of my Manhattan life.

MAC   If you can't come up with $1400, you have to be out by Tuesday. If you can scrape together that amount, you can stay 'til next Tuesday.

ROMY   A lot can happen in a day.

MAC   Or a week.

ROMY   You don't have to let them know I'm staying.

MAC   Security and construction will see you and report you.

ROMY   I'll hide in another part of the building until they're gone. You can tip me off.

MAC   It won't work. Let's go to the basement. The stuff you don't want goes in the trash.

ROMY   Just like an eviction in the South.

MAC   Worse. Manhattan's ground zero for COVID. Put on the gloves. They're by the masks. You don't know where COVID is in the building.

The scene switches to the basement.

MAC   Your stuff is over there.

ROMY   I used to be anal about my belongings. Now, I'm a homeless person. My life is in garbage bags. Eww. This is a jumbled mess!

MAC   What did you expect? Neatly folded dresses?

Silence.

ROMY   I'm not dead. Whoever it was that attacked me could have killed me. I am grateful. Thank you. You saved me. (*pause*) This is an APOCAPYLPSE.

MAC Here. Unused bags to take what you want. I have to make rounds. I'll be back in a bit.

ROMY But what about my dishes and my TV and, and jewelry and Warhol books.

MAC This is it. The rest was stolen and smashed.

ROMY I hope my jewelry box is here. Uh. wedding rings. I have to remember what's missing. Why can't I remember?

MAC You can always make an insurance claim.

ROMY I have no insurance. I'll make a claim against the company for not securing the building and sue for damages for my trauma and PTSD and memory loss and stolen property.

MAC Good luck with that.

Mac leaves. Romy rummages through the garbage bags.

ROMY I could weep. (*rummages*) Oh, the dress I wore to the New York Film Festival gala. And the Gucci bag that Charlie bought me. (*pause*) No jewelry box. These are ripped. Fuck! Here's my leather pants. Where is it? (*pause*) I remember. The box was in the closet's hiding place. Did they pull it down? Is it completely wrecked? One more precious thing I lost. If I see what's left of my apartment, I'll collapse. (*pause*) But the signed Warhol book.I have to see for myself. It's my life. I have to see. I have to know. I can't be afraid. I can't.

Romy leaves. Scene switches so Romy who stands at the door of her apartment which swings on its hinges. She pushes in and looks around. She investigates and finds nothing has changed.

ROMY It's the same. The floor, my bed, the kitchen, the same. My dishes are here. My closet? YES! It's here. (*rummages*) My jewelry box. Interview Magazine. The Warhol book. It's all here. I was right! "Baby, I'm a Firework! I'll show you what I'm really worth."

MAC enters. He quietly watches her sing and dance.

ROMY   I'll make 'em go, "Oh, oh, oh. Baby, I'm a firework! I'm a firework!?" The nightmare has ended. THE NIGHTMARE HAS ENDED.

MAC   NO! It's just beginning. Why are you here?

ROMY   You bastard. You bastard. I'll kill you. Let me smash your face.

Romy attacks, pummels Mac throughout the dialogue. Mac puts up a weak defense.

MAC   Stop! STOP OWWW. Let me explain. OWWW.

ROMY   If I had that gun I'd misfire it in your eye. I'm going to HURT YOU FOR LYING TO ME! LIAR! LIAR!

Romy slaps him in the face.

MAC   I did it to keep you safe.

ROMY   You said my place was WRECKED.

MAC   It will be.

ROMY   THEY'LL NEVER GET ME OUT. You FUCK! I'm pressing charges.

MAC   Have you learned nothing?

ROMY   I learned the lengths companies go to, to make boat loads of money. They hurt people. Destroy their lives. And they have their Adolf Eichmanns TO HELP THEM DO IT. Without warped people like you, they COULDN'T BE TERRORISTS.

MAC I'm sorry. I know what it looks like.

ROMY What it looks like? What! It! Is! You said the nightmare is just beginning? No, liar. YOUR nightmare is just beginning.

MAC This is not my real job.

ROMY You TRICKED ME. And I BELIEVED YOU. Now, who's trespassing. Get the fuck out. Out! OUT!

MAC It's good you believed me. It gave us time. I'm not with them.

ROMY YOU FAKE! You're their good little storm trooper.

MAC My identification badge. This is who I work for.
Mac takes out his ID

ROMY It doesn't matter. Once a fake always a fake.

Mac shoves the ID in her face.

MAC LOOK AT IT! You don't make up one of these.

ROMY You're full of shit. I'm not falling for it.

MAC Metal threads. Look! These can't be counterfeited.

ROMY You're with the company but don't work for them? B.S. (*pause*) I don't get it.

MAC You're a smart woman. Think.

ROMY You're fronting Luxurious Living?

MAC Bullseye.

ROMY (*pause*) Why?

MAC You've spent days brutalized in their world of hell. And you're asking me that?

ROMY But you said, they control the city and with COVID, and, (*realizes*) the attack. You're a part of it!

MAC I wasn't there. (*listening*) I didn't know what they were planning.

ROMY It's hard to hear the truth, isn't it you, Goebbels.

MAC Shushhh. Someone's on the stairs. The closet. Quick.

ROMY I will not!

MAC Hide in the closet. Whoever is coming will say what's going on. I'm playing along.

ROMY You fucking fuck. You will not screw me ever again.

MAC I showed you the badge. They don't expect you to be here. They think you're in the basement.

ROMY Now you're on the hot seat. Good! Let's see what you do if they find me here.

MAC You're a witness to their fraud. You want to be hit over the head again? This time, you won't wake up.

Mac pushes her in the closet.

ROMY (*pause*) You better not be.you better not.

MAC Don't come out until I signal.

Mac goes to the living room. Romy listens in the closet. Bob comes in with Sal, both masked.

BOB Change of plans.

SAL The hold on renovations is lifted. She in the basement or 5C?

MAC Basement.

SAL She has to be out of the building.

MAC She can come up with the money to stay in 5C.

SAL They're starting tomorrow. Our guy in the building department got what he wanted. He's made up all the papers. Date's for tomorrow. She's out today.

MAC She has nowhere to go.

SAL Not our problem.

BOB I'm on overtime. You want me to get measurements?

MAC Take a break and come back.

SAL You don't tell him. I tell him. (*pause*) Take a break.

BOB Whatever. It's your dime.

Bob leaves

SAL Whatta ya gotta tell me?

MAC You don't want her to make trouble, right?

SAL She can't do nothin' 'cause we got the Mayor's Office to OK everything. She goes. Company don't want her around to see what's going on. Paperwork says it's legal.

MAC I told her the apartment was stripped.

SAL   Different if she sees us doing it. That's eyewitness testimony. That's hard evidence. They don't want no eyewitnesses. They need an empty building.

MAC   Just for a few days.

SAL   What's your problem? I said today. Handle it. They don't care how you do it. Get rid of her.

MAC   What if I can't?

SAL   Then the other security team takes over. If she disappears, no one cares. You said she has no family.

MAC   She has a friend.

SAL   Don't give me what for. If you can't get her out, the other team handles it. They won't be so nice this time. She won't wake up. She'll go with the bums they're burying in Potter's Field cause no one's claiming bodies.

MAC   Let management tell her.

SAL   They stay out of it.

MAC   So then, it's on you.

SAL   No. It's on you. I'm your boss.

MAC   I quit.

SAL   You're in too deep. You're a part of it.

MAC   Don't lay that on me. I'm not a heavy hitter here. Just a go-between. Your thugs did the dirty work.

SAL   I did what I was told.

MAC   Using your sources and methods.

SAL That's what they pay me for. But if I go up the river with a long sentence, I sing like a canary and take them with me.

MAC You're not getting paid enough to go to prison.

SAL Who says I'm going?

MAC Just sayin,' if you make mistakes.

SAL Mistakes? You pull anything stupid, you'll end up in Potter's Field with her. They're not checking for identification, I hear. Just getting rid of the corpses so they don't contaminate the city. If fire pits were legal, they'd be burning the bodies.

MAC Yeah, yeah.

SAL I have to be somewhere. If she don't leave, let me know.

Sal stomps out. Mac goes to the closet to get Romy.

ROMY Has that bastard gone? On a respirator? Christ.

MAC Part of the lie to scare you.

ROMY You're a bastard. I was actually feeling sorry for him.

MAC I lie. Good undercover work requires it. Never feel sorry for a thug.

ROMY But they can't do this.

MAC Of course they can.

ROMY But it's not legal.

MAC Of course it is.

ROMY It's against state laws, rental control board.

MAC Laws are useless if no one's enforcing them.

ROMY So what are you saying?

MAC If you don't leave, you'll be a casualty of COVID.

ROMY I don't have COVID.

MAC Did you hear the man? No one autopsies the bodies. If you turn up dead, it's COVID. Potter's Field is waiting.

ROMY But all I want to do is live here in my place!

MAC Not ever again.

ROMY But I can scrape together some money for.

Bob returns.

BOB OK. I figure you're all talked. hey what the fuck?

MAC I can explain.

BOB You said she was in the basement. (*loudly*) Sal. Hey Sal. You gotta see this.

Bob goes to leave.

MAC I said I can explain.

Mac punches Bob in the face. Bob collapses unconscious.

ROMY Christ. He fell like a stone. Was that necessary?

MAC Get your stuff. We've gotta get outta here. COME ON.

ROMY I'm not going back to the basement. I'm staying.

MAC Now! You'll be happy when you see where we're going.

ROMY BULLSHIT.

MAC Come on! You want me to kick him in the head, so he never wakes up?

ROMY All right, all right. Help me get my stuff from the closet.

Lights dim on Romy and Mac taking Romy's things from her closet.

MAC Now! You'll be happy when you see where we're going.

MAC Come on! You want me to kick him in the head, so he never wakes up?

Scene 5

A few hours later, in the evening. Dree and Bill's Upper West Side building. The hallway. Mac and Romy carry garbage bags of her stuff and drop it in front of Bill's door.

ROMY Do you or don't you live here? You are so weird.

MAC You're finally safe. I'll be back.

ROMY It's like I never left. I'm still homeless. It's still a nightmare. Bill! Bill! Open up. You can't hide. I know you're in there. Bill! Bill!

BILL You! Whadda you want? I lost money on those stinking football tips. That Mark guy's an asshole.

ROMY I, I, I'm sorry about that. Bill, I need your help.

BILL No. No help. You're toxic. Besides, my wife left me.

ROMY A friend of yours said.

BILL (*loudly*) I said my wife left me. No more women. You women are trouble. Trouble! Go away! My wife left me! Left me!

Mac joins Romy at the door to confront Bill.

MAC It's OK. You can drop the act.

BILL (*real voice*) Did you get what we needed?

MAC Yeah. I'm pleased. I think it's a start.

ROMY What the fuck is going on?

MAC Recorded it on my phone. Romy has to stay with us. She's our evidence. Lucky she's alive.

ROMY (*shocked*) You? You? You?

BILL Me, me, me. (*pause*) What? For the first time in your life, you have nothing to say? Ha, ha, ha.

ROMY I can't believe it. you're working with him?

BILL Is that a problem for you? If you have the courage, you'll be working with us, too.

MAC You've just been made an official whistleblower.

ROMY (*still shocked*) You mean, you mean, you mean…

BILL Companies have been fucking with tenants for some years now. COVID just gave them carte blanche.

Bill waves Romy and Mac into the apartment. He puts the garbage bags of stuff by the door.

MAC We're going after criminal companies and the corrupt in the New York City building department and related agencies. It's your chance to make a difference.

BILL We have a long way to go.

ROMY So my apartment is, is

BILL Your coffin. If you go back there, it won't just be an apartment you lose. You help us, we indict them.

MAC You can initiate a lawsuit to make yourself whole.

ROMY I tried so hard. They've got too much money and power.

MAC And they've got friends in high places.

ROMY   The apartment was my inheritance from my family.

BILL   There's the recording and other evidence we've got. We're still investigating.

MAC   You're a witness. All they did to get you out, the rats, roaches, shutting off the electricity and heat, the attack. Threatening your life. You confirm how these companies operate. They wipe out the laws. Friends in high places legitimize evictions and push delays and decades-long lawsuits until the tenants give up.

BILL   COVID is making the situation worse. But the governor put that moratorium on evictions. There's hope.

ROMY   Not for me. I lost.

BILL   They'll be charged. Mac's with the Feds. I'm the AGs office. Others are on the joint task force investigation.

MAC   It's not every day you're part of a sting operation and work with a good-looking guy.

BILL   Yeah. When I put off this rough, dorky exterior and clean up, I'm hot!

MAC   Yeah, right.ha, ha, ha.

ROMY   I thought you were crazy. You're a great actor.

MAC   You have to be when you're undercover.

BILL   But I am a hoarder. He tries to keep me under control.

ROMY   I know just what needs to go.

BILL   Don't touch nothin.' This is museum quality stuff, here.

MAC   The look on your face! Ha, ha, ha. You fell for it again

ROMY   If you let me stay, I'll testify in court and end your hoarding.

BILL   Yeah? No. If you throw stuff out, I'll bring it back in or find replacements.

MAC   Leave things as they are, or he'll go berserk. Ha, ha.

BILL   The stuff you left back there, make a list.

MAC   You stay here until COVID is over. After, the bureau will make other arrangements for you for a place to live.

BILL   We'll set you up with a lawyer to civilly sue Luxurious Living. And we'll go after them criminally.

MAC   Tomorrow, write down each incident. End with the conversation you overheard between Sal, me and Bob.

ROMY   I can't believe it.

BILL   With all the dark money coming into housing in NYC and elsewhere, it's like Schrödinger's cat. Real estate is being used to wash dirty money. Impossible to prove. No affordable housing. With the Governor's moratorium on eviction the shit is hitting the fan. Landlords and companies screaming lost profits and higher expenses to be COVID compliant. The business contingent wants Cuomo OUT! It will be worse when the moratorium lifts. Tenants will be screaming about crazy rent hikes. Housing will skyrocket and be even less affordable. Something has to be done. We've got to hold them accountable.at least try.

ROMY   You left me at Schrödinger's cat

MAC   Put a cat and plutonium in a sealed box. Is the cat alive or dead? It's both until you open the box and find out.

BILL In other words, we have no way of knowing what's going on until we open the box and investigate, have grand juries, find whistleblowers, to give testimony for criminal indictments.

ROMY It's like Pandora's box, too. COVID unleashed something we can't wrap our minds around or put back in the box. Will things ever be restored?

BILL Unlikely. It'll take years.

MAC You don't want restored. You want better. It takes time. Indictments send a message.

BILL Until they find a way to get around us again. For criminals, the scofflaw wealthy and their crooked attorneys and bought politicians, there's one thousand ways to break the law.

ROMY (*pause*) I'm thirsty and starving. Got any of that great wine you gave me when I was, when, two months ago…wow. When I met you two, I never suspected. Seems so long ago.

BILL I'm a much better actor than he is.

Bill gets a bottle of red wine and four glasses. He opens it then pours.

MAC Fuck you, too. Didn't you hear her? She never suspected!

ROMY I thought you and Sal were thick as thieves.

MAC Yeah. No.

ROMY Hey. You never gave my Derringer back.

MAC You pull a gun on law enforcement, they shoot first, then do the paperwork.

ROMY I could have used it against Sal.

MAC He did security before this job. Pulling a gun on him is an excuse to use his Glock.

BILL OK. Today we celebrate. Tomorrow, you write up your testimony. I'll get some snacks.

ROMY So you do have a wine cooler?

MAC We each have our own wine coolers.

Bill and Mac clear things and arrange the wine and snacks. Romy phones Dree.

DREE (*coughing*) ARGH! Hack! What?

ROMY You sound better.

DREE I am better.

ROMY It was that Elderberry and zinc and fresh squeezed lemon and liquids.

DREE And calling up Boone's wife and telling her about his love nest in Manhattan. Just to hear her screaming at Boone about some Black bitch mistress was the elixir I needed.

ROMY Girl, you did not!

DREE I most certainly did and the next day. I felt 90%. I just have a cough.

ROMY We are definitely celebrating. Go to your door and open it.

DREE Why?

ROMY Just do it.

Dree and Romy open the apartment doors and look down the hall.

ROMY (screams) HEY! SURPRISE!

DREE Oh my God. What are you doing?

ROMY Great news. Come over.

Bill and Mac join Romy in the hallway. Bill waves.

DREE Hey Bill. I better not. Still sick. What? Tell me! What?

ROMY I'm staying with Bill and Mac.

DREE Mac? The Mac?

Mac gives the wine in the glasses to Bill and Romy and gives one at arm's length to Dree.

MAC You're Dree. Romy told me about you.

DREE Hey Mac. Don't keep me in suspense. Tell me.

MAC Gruesome story, hopeful ending.

BILL Manhattan real estate needs regulation of dark foreign money to stop the Wild West.

DREE Cuomo put in the moratorium on evictions. I'm OK.

BILL For now.

ROMY Maybe you can eventually move in with us.

BILL and MAC Hold on. Wait a minute. I don't know about that.

ROMY A toast to us. We celebrate going after criminals and living together. It's how to maximize space in Manhattan.

They clink glasses.

Lights out.

The End.

181

◊ ⟡ I'll Take Manhattan ⟡ ◊